SHORT WALKS

West Kent Pubs

Bea Cowan

COUNTRYSIDE BOOKS
NEWBURY, BERKSHIRE

COUNTRYSIDE BOOKS
3 Catherine Road
Newbury, Berkshire

ISBN 1 85306 347 9

Designed by Mon Mohan
Cover illustration by Colin Doggett
Photographs by the author

Produced through MRM Associates Ltd., Reading
Typeset by The Midlands Book Typesetting Company, Loughborough
Printed by Woolnough Bookbinding, Irthlingborough

Contents

Publisher's Note

We hope that you obtain considerable enjoyment from this book; great care has been taken in its preparation. However, changes of landlord and actual closures are sadly not uncommon. Likewise, although at the time of publication all routes followed public rights of way or permitted paths, diversion orders can be made and permissions withdrawn.

We cannot of course be held responsible for such diversion orders and any inaccuracies in the text which result from these or any other changes to the routes nor any damage which might result from walkers trespassing on private property. However, we are anxious that all details covering the walks and the pubs are kept up to date and would therefore welcome information from readers which would be relevant to future editions.

Area map showing locations of the walks.

Introduction

This collection of 20 circular walks in West Kent aims to show you the outstanding variety and beauty of one part of the South-East. Kent has long been known as the garden of England, a county of orchards and hop farms. But there is much more. The Thames marshland of the Hoo peninsula, to the north, is a place of remote expanses and wide skies, an important area for migrant birds in winter. On the North Downs, an Area of Outstanding Natural Beauty, you find the wonderful flora of the chalk downland. Further south, the Greensand Ridge gives splendid views, while, stretching along the Kent-Sussex border and spreading well into mid-Kent, the High Weald, another AONB, offers a unique landscape of rolling slopes, steep-sided ghylls and high viewpoints.

As you walk in West Kent you will discover this rich blend, created by nature and man, a patchwork of fields and pasture, separated by ancient and coppiced woodland, shaws or shelter belts.

Scattered across the landscape you will see the houses and villages. You will come across the oasthouses, the Wealden, half-timbered houses, the weatherboarding and the hung tiles. In many of these places important episodes in English history took place. Not far away are the churches, which often record the history. Nearby you will almost always find the inn.

The walks in this book are circular, starting and finishing at a pub. All are short, the longest being 3½ miles, the shortest a comfortable 1½ miles.

We have chosen the pubs, on which the walks are based, for their own characteristics, their welcome, their style and atmosphere, and often their history. All are places where you may happily take a family, old or young – and the food is good. As well as the ales and other alcoholic drinks mentioned in the text, coffee and fruit juices are always available.

Most pubs offer car parking for patrons. If you wish to leave your car there while you walk, it is courteous to ask the landlord's permission beforehand.

The network of footpaths throughout Kent is outstanding. There are many of them and they are well maintained. All of the walks described are along well-trodden tracks. Usually, they are well signed, either with a simple yellow arrow, or with the logo of a long distance path or a circular walk. From time to time, however, the route may take a less usual turning, to include a viewpoint or to fit in with the right of way. In this case the instructions are clear.

Some of the walks link up with country parks. Their establishment in the last decade has led to the development of many circular walks arcund them. The visitors centres often have interesting and informative displays, as well as refreshments for all ages. Other walks touch on one of the fine long distance paths which cross Kent; the Saxon Shore Way, the North Downs Way, the Greensand Way, the High Weald Walk or the Sussex Border Path. Two shorter, medium distance paths also figure, the Darent Valley Walk and the Eden Valley Walk.

All the routes follow carefully established rights of way. Under normal circumstances you should follow them faithfully. You may sometimes find a farmer has ploughed and planted over one of these. In this case you may walk across. Alternatively, you may follow the edge of the field, known as the headland, to join the path further on. If you find a path impossibly obstructed, please do inform the Highways Officer, Highways and Transportation Department, Kent County Council, Springfield, Maidstone, Kent ME14 2LX.

The relevant Ordnance Survey map for each walk is helpful and interesting. Grid references are included, with the number of the map required. The Landranger 1:50 000 gives an overall picture, while the Pathfinder 1:25 000 series is the ideal walking map.

Good boots are recommended for all winter walking. Where boots are mentioned in the text they are doubly recommended.

I should like to thank all those who have helped me in the research for this selection of walks in West Kent. In particular I am indebted to Roger Lambert of Kent County Council, who has done so much to open up the long distance paths of the region, and to Chris Wade, also of Kent County Council, for his help in checking the rights of way. I should also like to thank John Guy and Anne Hopley of Rochester-upon-Medway City Council for their help with the walk from Cliffe on the Hoo peninsula.

I am grateful to all those who have walked, marked and noted the footpaths before me, in particular the following councils – Sevenoaks Borough Council, Tonbridge and Malling Borough Council, Tunbridge Wells Borough Council, Tenterden Borough Council and the parish councils of Cranbrook and Hawkhurst. I also acknowledge the help given by the landlords of all the pubs included.

Bea Cowan
Spring 1995

Westerham
The George and Dragon

The small market town of Westerham, between the North Downs and the Greensand Ridge, makes a fascinating base in an area of fine walking. Its green, the winding High Street, with its handsome buildings on either side, the many antique shops and the nearby historic houses add interest and variety to any walk.

The George and Dragon is situated in the centre of Westerham, on the north side of Market Square. It offers all the atmosphere and history of a traditional coaching inn. In 1758 its oak beams witnessed General Wolfe's last night in England before he left for Quebec. Today regulars and visitors are all welcome, children and families included. A pleasant carvery completes the scene.

The choice of bar food is wide. As a special dish you may find sweet and sour pork or cottage pie. Boeuf bourguignonne figures and the winter stew is highly recommended in the appropriate season. You may also choose the carvery roast, as either a one or three course meal. The real ale drinker will find a good and changing selection – Theakston Best Bitter, Mild or Old Peculier, for example. Those who fancy cider can drink Scrumpy Jack or Strongbow on draught or choose from the bottled ciders moved in rotation. The inn is open all day from 11 am

to 11 pm on weekdays. Food is available between 12 noon and 3.30 pm and from 6 pm to 9 pm. Sunday opening is from 12 noon to 3.30 pm and from 7 pm to 10.30 pm.
Telephone: 01959 563245.

How to get there: Westerham lies on the A25, west of Sevenoaks and south of Bromley, between junctions 5 and 6 of the M25. The inn stands on the corner of the A25 and the A233 Bromley road.

Parking: You may drive under the archway to the inn's car park at the back. Public car parks include one at the corner 200 yards north, down London Road, on the right. Another, larger, park lies 500 yards east, beyond St Mary's church, towards Sevenoaks.

Length of the walk: 3½ miles. OS maps: Landranger 187 Dorking, Reigate and Crawley, Pathfinder 1208 Sevenoaks and Westerham (inn GR 446541).

This walk reveals some of the immense variety of this part of the Greensand Ridge. You walk between open fields, with fine views of the North Downs. Then you take a broad track through woodland on the slopes of a steep combe. You return down the widening valley, beside the upper waters of the river Darent.

The Walk
Leave the inn by the front doorway, turn left to the green, with its statues of General Wolfe and Sir Winston Churchill. Cross the road where you see a small central reservation. Almost immediately to your right you will see some steps rising into Water Lane. Go up the steps and follow the sign directing you towards the Greensand Way.
Follow the path for 200 yards until it narrows by a bridge, cross over a stone barrier and continue along a tarmac path between fences. Turn right at the kissing gate and walk 400 yards, with the river Darent on your right, to the next bridge. Turn left and follow the track past a house, Park Lodge, with hung tiles on the upper storey. Turn immediately right, over a stile, then go up the hill to another stile. Once past the woods which lie to your right you will get some excellent views of the North Downs.
Below these woods, but well hidden from this point, lies Squerryes Court. Continue along a path between fences to the next stile, cross a small field planted with trees, then go over a stile, first to a sandy path then, following an arrow, straight ahead into woodland.
Ignoring all side paths, continue ahead along a broad woodland track. The ground slopes fairly steeply to your left to reveal a deeply cut

9

Statue of Sir Winston Churchill, Westerham.

valley. This surprisingly rugged terrain provided a good vantage point and protection for early Celts. Remains of an Iron Age fort have been found on the far slope. After ¹/₂ mile, as you begin to drop downhill, you will begin to see the Greensand Way signs. After ¹/₄ mile more you will reach a metal gate and stile. Cross the stile and continue past Kent Hatch Lodge for 100 yards. Turn left into a small clearing, following the Greensand Way sign, then bend right. You will also see a Greensand Way marker on your right as you go uphill.

Turn left when you reach a broad sandy track. Continue, as this becomes an old driveway, between the beech trees, rhododendron ponticum and bracken which cover this part of Crockhamhill Common. About ¹/₂ mile after the turning, the woodland ends and you pass a white lodge on your left, at the corner of a field. Go ahead over a stile, and walk along a narrow path fenced off from the field. A steep bank rises above you.

At the end, where several ways meet, turn left over a stile into the field and head towards the trees along a grassy track. A little lower down the slope, to your right, you see the river Darent, which has risen on the slopes behind you to begin its course to the Thames near Dartford (the Darent ford). You now follow the river's course back to Westerham, though keeping well above it in places.

Cross a stile where the path meets woods and walk beside the trees

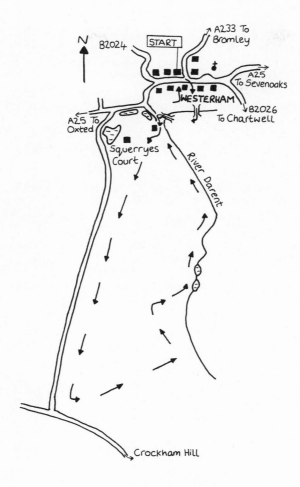

along a ledge above the valley. The old fort lies above you. Cross another stile, at a large metal gate, to a crossing of ways, then at the far right-hand corner of this junction go over a stile set at an angle, into a field. Walk down the right side, a fence on your right separating you from a broad, sandy track. Join a field path at the end and go past a part of the river which has been dammed for fish. This is an attractive part of the valley, with woods rising on your right and fields on your left. You pass more ponds as you go. Eventually you come to a wooden gate with an elderly stile beside it.

The path now takes you back to Park Lodge. Here you go over a stile and retrace your steps to the Darent bridge. This time go past the bridge. Just before the long, low cottage ahead, follow the arrow pointing diagonally to the right. Then take a narrow path between houses. A little alley at the end takes you down some steps, between Berry's Cottage and Blank Cottage. Cross the lane and continue along another narrow way, between fence and wall.

After $1/8$ mile turn left into the car park of the King's Arms. The archway leads you back to Market Square and the George and Dragon.

Places of interest nearby

To the east of Westerham stands 17th-century *Quebec House*, where Sir James Wolfe grew up. This National Trust property is open from April to the end of October. Telephone: 01959 562206.

To the south lies *Chartwell* (NT), one-time home of Sir Winston Churchill, open April to October. Telephone: 01732 866368.

Squerryes Court, in the grounds of which Wolfe received his first commission, contains a fine collection of 18th-century paintings and has an interesting and recently-restored formal garden. It is open from April to the end of September. Telephone: 01959 563118.

2 Godden Green
The Buck's Head

Godden Green lies along winding lanes to the east of Sevenoaks. The village green, circled by old houses, and a small village pond beside the inn combine to provide an air of peace and tranquillity. The Buck's Head, dating from the 16th century, is set beside the pond, looking over the green. It has a strongly traditional atmosphere and welcomes walkers of all ages.

Meals cater for every taste. Among the well-prepared bar food are jacket potatoes with a variety of fillings. Instead, you can enjoy the Buck's Head smokies or have king prawns in filo pastry. The excellent three course Sunday roast, taken in the Antler's Restaurant, undoubtedly calls for a good walk afterwards. There are special portions, with ice-cream always added at the end, for children – who are welcome to eat in the restaurant. You will find an interesting range of real ales – the inn's own Buck's Head Bitter, John Smith's and Old Speckled Hen, alongside Boddingtons, Wadworth 6X, Courage Best and Directors. Lagers include Miller Pilsner, Foster's, Kronenbourg and Budweiser. You can get Blackthorn Dry cider on draught. For those who prefer, there are all the juices imaginable. There is a selection of wines, named by their region. The opening times are from 11.15 am to 2.30 pm and

from 6 pm to 11 pm. On Sunday the inn is open between 12 noon and 3 pm, with food served all that time. On Sunday evening the bar opens from 7 pm to 10.30 pm. Food is served every day from 12 noon to 2 pm and 6 pm to 9 pm, except on Sunday and Monday nights.
Telephone: 01732 761330.

How to get there: Take the A21 south at junction 5 of the M25, then the first exit left as the motorway ends. Go east towards Sevenoaks and Maidstone. Turn right ¾ mile after the junction with the A225 (known as the Bat and Ball junction) and follow the signs to Godden Green.

Parking: There is some parking in front of the inn. Otherwise, you may park beside the green.

Length of the walk: 3 miles. OS maps: Landranger 188 Maidstone and The Weald of Kent, Pathfinder 1208 Sevenoaks and Westerham (inn GR 553552).

This walk takes you across Knole Park to Knole House. You enter the park through woodland, and soon find yourself on some of the highest ground of the area, with splendid views across the Low Weald to the North Downs. Following a metalled track you come to the house, go round its perimeter, then return by a different route over gentle, turf tracks to get the full flavour of this historic parkland.
Dogs must be kept on a lead in Knole Park.

The Walk
Turn left when you leave the pub, then turn immediately left again into a driveway which takes you past stabling to a wooden gate. Cross the road and enter a metalled track which leads through woodland to a large gate at the entrance to Knole Park.

Follow the road as it winds across the park and downhill. You will see golfers on the golf course and many of the deer that roam here freely. After ¾ mile two other tracks join. Veer left and continue on the main footpath, an oak-lined avenue known as Duchess Walk. Pass a walled compound on your left and walk up to the northern corner of the house. The Brewhouse tearooms (National Trust) are on your left. Turn right towards the car parking area, then left, to reach the front of the house. Owned by Lord Sackville and the largest private house in the country, Knole House was first built in 1456. Its clock tower, Dutch gables and chimneys are all distinctive features. The state rooms contain an outstanding collection of furniture, silver and tapestries as well as portraits by Reynolds and Gainsborough.

To leave, walk past the front of the house and continue to the corner

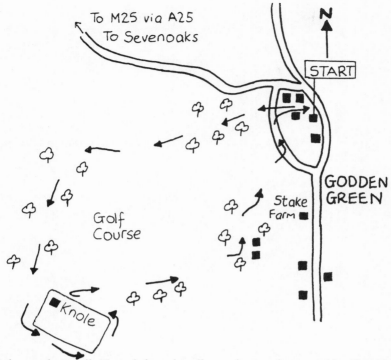

To M25 via A25
To Sevenoaks

N

START

GODDEN GREEN

Golf Course

Stake Farm

Knole

of the garden wall. Turn left and walk up the south-west side. Turn left again and walk along the south-east side, then left once more to return to the tearoom corner. By circling the house in this way, you will have some excellent glimpses of the south-western façade and clock tower.

Before you return to the tearoom you will see a large wooden gate set at an angle into the garden wall. Here there is a grassy track which doubles back to your right at 45° from your path. Follow this and cross a line of young beeches 40 yards ahead. Continue towards rougher grass, which soon flanks the path. Cross a narrow, single ride and proceed to the sign which warns you of the danger of the golf course.

On the far side of the fairway you will see the roof tops of the golf club. Look carefully to your left as you cross. On the other side of the fairway you enter another area of rougher grass. Cross another sandy track and continue until you come to the 14th tee. Do not be surprised if you see the deer helping the greenkeeper to keep the grass down on the tee here or elsewhere. The seat placed here is for golfers, not walkers, so keep going. About 40 yards ahead you will come to a metalled track. Cross and make for a cluster of oaks, seven on the left-hand side in bracken, forming a semi-circle, three in a line on the right.

Drop to a small valley, then cross a broad, grassy ride, and go straight uphill along a grassy path, with bracken on either side. You will pass a tall chestnut on your right. Take a line on a beech tree on the left-hand side of the track which looks dead but is still managing to grow from the right-hand side. Walk under its limbs, and pass a small pond on your right, surrounded with grasses. A small hawthorn grows at an angle over it on the far left corner.

Knole Park was devastated by the hurricane of 1987. Indeed, six of the town's seven oaks were lost. The dead wood now provides good habitats for insects. Knole Park is host to a wide variety of insect-life and is a Side of Special Scientific Interest. Just before some fallen stumps you reach a narrow, grassy ride which goes slightly left to join a mesh wire fence and run beside it towards woodland. Pass between two very tall trees, which flank the pathway, an oak on your left, a beech, with remarkable gnarled roots, on your right. Continue down to a steep slope to a gate and enter a broad track between fences.

Turn left at the bottom by the house and continue up the slope, for ¼ mile, past sports fields on the right and grazing on your left, to a junction. Turn left and walk 350 yards until you reach the gate by the stables. Turn right and return to Godden Green and the Buck's Head.

Places of interest nearby

The main entrance to *Knole House* (National Trust) is in Sevenoaks itself, south of the junction of the London Road and the High Street. Knole House is open from April to the end of October, on Wednesday, Friday, Saturday and Sunday, also bank holiday Mondays, from 11 am to 5 pm, and on Thursdays from 2 pm to 5 pm.

3 Shipbourne
The Chaser

Built in the 1880s in the estate-style for Fairlawne House, ³/₄ mile up the road, the Chaser stands back from the A227, opposite a large common. Its name is said to come from the connection with the late Peter Cazalet who ran the National Hunt stables nearby and who was trainer to the Queen Mother's horses. Colourful and immaculate hanging baskets decorate the verandah. Inside there is a welcome for all, including dogs. Old hunting pictures hang on the walls.

Food may be taken in the bar or snug area, the courtyard, on the verandah or, on warm days, at tables set on the lawn next to St Giles' church. There is also a restaurant with a beamed, vaulted ceiling and panelled walls. The menu of home-made bar food changes daily and provides for all needs. You could start with stuffed aubergines, then have skate with capers or steak and kidney pie and finish with banoffi pie. For those setting out on their walk the cheese ploughman's makes a good alternative. The main lunch menu includes grilled halibut with prawns and garlic, sauté of pigeon breast with red wine sauce, rack of lamb and rosemary. For dinner you could choose pike terrine. On bank holidays a barbecue is held in the garden. To quench your thirst you will find Harveys Best Bitter and Shepherd Neame Master Brew and Guinness as well as Dry Blackthorn cider. Hürlimann's lager also figures, alongside Carling Black Label. There is an extensive selection of wine from round the world. The list from Australia includes a Penfold Semillon Chardonnay. You may also drink local wine from Sedlescombe in Sussex. The bar is open from 11 am to 3 pm and from 6 pm to 11 pm. Sunday 12 noon to 3 pm and 7 pm to 10.30 pm. Food is served every day from 12 noon to 2 pm and from 7 pm to 9.30 pm.

Telephone: 01732 810360.

How to get there: The Chaser is on the A227 Gravesend to Tonbridge road, 3³/₄ miles south of Borough Green.

Parking: You may park behind and beside the pub. You can also park beside the common, away from the main road.

Length of the walk: 3¹/₂ miles. OS maps: Landranger 188 Maidstone and The Weald of Kent, Pathfinder 1208 Sevenoaks and Westerham (inn GR 592522).

The walk leads you through the churchyard of St Giles', across fields and up the slopes of the Greensand Ridge to give marvellous views southwards to the High Weald before returning along part of the long distance Greensand Way itself. Close to the walk stands the moated medieval manor house of Ightham Mote, one of the loveliest of the National Trust's properties and easily reached from the walk or as a separate visit afterwards.

Boots are recommended.

The Walk

Turn left out of the Chaser, go through the lychgate of St Giles' church, take the path to the right-hand side of the church, then go through the kissing gate in the stone wall on the far side. As you pass the church look up to the delightful gargoyles which fly outwards from the four corners of the tower.

A tall fingerpost on the far side of the wall shows the various walks in this region. Follow the sign leading straight on and cross the first field to a gap in the hedge, then cross the next field, which rises slightly towards the right-hand corner of the woodland ahead. Lines of grey willows cross the estate at many points. Each year two are felled and made into cricket bats.

At the corner of the wood go through the gate and enter. Almost immediately, you will see a division of tracks. Take the path leading to the right. Follow a broad, grassy woodland ride uphill for about 200 yards then fork left. At the top of the slope, where another ride

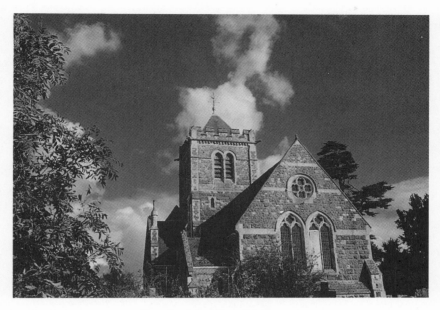

Church of St Giles, Shipbourne.

joins from the left, you get a marvellous view down to the High Weald. Follow the path as it bears right, ignoring all the side tracks, and go downhill towards the oasts at Budd's Green.

Turn right onto the small road. Almost immediately you will see a broad double-barred gate on your left. Cross the stile beside it and walk at 45° to a broad gap in the nearby hedge line. Turn left by the tall oak. Leave the hedge on your left and walk for 300 yards towards the corner of woodland, a few degrees to the right of the hedge line. Cross a narrow bridge and go ahead to the next corner of trees, now going slightly uphill.

Skirt the trees and follow the path round to the left to the edge of a stream. Cross another field-ditch with a low bridge. At an oak tree the path now stops hugging the hedge line and makes its way towards a narrow stile with one good, broad step, beside a hazel tree on the right. Turn slightly left and continue uphill towards the recently restored house with its three dormer windows, hung tiles, and ragstone walls. Before you reach the path you will notice, beside the hedge at an opening into a field further left, clear signs of damper ground where a spring emerges along a fault line in the underlying rock. Although the reason for the boots, this need not be too worrying. Leave the spring to your left, make first for the tufty, grassy outcrop, then for the stile in the fence.

19

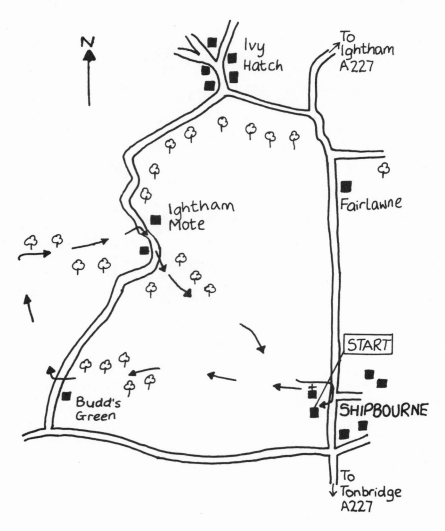

Cross the stile and turn right onto a well-made track. Along this stretch you will have a series of views towards the High Weald, which should more than compensate for any sogginess underfoot in the last field. In the track you will find occasional pieces of greensand. This is not green but almost black, where the mineral, glauconite, has darkened through weathering. After ½ mile you will begin to see ahead of you the Jacobean chimneys of Ightham Mote, which nestles in a small valley. At Mote Farm turn left, past the granary, then right, onto the road.

Ightham Mote is a unique moated manor house. Built in the 14th century, it was developed and embellished over several centuries. Now you can see a 14th-century great hall, a Tudor chapel and a Jacobean drawing room built round a central courtyard. The whole is surmounted by a gate tower and encircled by a moat. If you wish to visit Ightham Mote while on the walk, turn left at the large gateway and follow the public footpath past the house and up the slope until you see car parking on your left. Turn left, then left again just after the hedge, to reach the entrance. For details of opening times, telephone 01732 810378.

To continue the walk, go along the road to where you see 'road curves' sign. Climb over a broad stile and follow the field headland, which runs beside a hedge next to the road, until you reach another stile, beside an old oak tree. Cross and make your way slightly uphill, leaving woodland on your left, to another stile at the top left-hand side of the next field. Turn left over this stile and follow a broad, woodland path until you reach a stile with one riser pointing straight ahead and leading into a field on a downhill slope. You will find a tall yellow marker standing to one side. Ahead lies Shipbourne church. Go down the slope, leaving a single oak on your left, to another oak ahead at the bottom. Swing left and make for the corner of a plantation hedged by conifers.

Go ahead to a broad track running at right angles ahead of you. Turn right, then continue straight ahead, leaving the hedge on your left. Follow the 'Alternative Footpath' sign rather than the Greensand Way over the stile across the field. A new fence made of unusually well-turned wood leads you round until you see a dovecote ahead. After about 100 yards cross a stile on the right at the corner of a field. This is the field you crossed further over at the beginning of the walk. Turn left along the fence line and make your way along to the kissing gate in the wall at the back of St Giles' church. The gargoyles are still there and the inn is still on the right as you go through the lychgate.

4 Eynsford
The Plough

Eynsford, in the Darent valley, is well known for its attractive ford over the river Darent as well as for the castle nearby. The Plough has an ideal position by the river. Children can paddle while parents enjoy their drink. An alehouse in the early 19th century, it retains its half-timbered façade. You can see it as it was in an old print inside. Now, much extended, the pub has two different dining areas and its old world style makes it a pleasant start to a walk in an area with a long history.

Here you can get the full range of standard dishes – chilli con carne, lasagne, roast chicken, for example. For a stronger taste there is a range of curries. Should you wish to eat lightly before your walk, jacket potatoes with a choice of fillings as well as soups, sandwiches and ploughman's lunches are all available. Puddings include chocolate fudge cake and fruit pie. The special dishes for the day on the chalkboard change daily. Children are welcome and smaller portions are served. To drink you will find Fremlins Bitter, Flowers Original, Boddingtons Bitter, Whitbread Best and Murphy's Irish Stout. The Fuggles Chocolate recalls an important variety of the hop plant. Lagers include Heineken and Stella Artois. The Plough is open all day from Monday to Saturday,

Viaduct near Eynsford.

from 10 am to 11 pm. On Sundays it is open from 12 noon to 3 pm and 7 pm to 10.30 pm. The restaurant is open on weekdays from 12 noon to 2.30 pm and 6 pm to 10.30 pm, on Saturday from 5.30 pm to 11 pm, and on Sunday from 10 am to 10.30 pm.
Telephone: 01322 862281.

How to get there: Eynsford lies on the A225 Dartford to Sevenoaks road. From the M25 at junction 3 head east towards Maidstone, Ashford and Dover on the A20. Some 650 yards after the roundabout-junction with the A225, turn right to Sevenoaks. Turn right in Eynsford village to 'Lullingstone Castle'. The Plough is beyond the bridge and ford, on the right.

Parking: There is a good car park at the back of the inn.

Length of the walk: 2 miles. OS maps: Landranger 177 East London area, Pathfinder 1192 Orpington (inn GR 539656).

This walk involves a short climb to take you up the slopes above the river Darent near Eynsford, past the impressive viaduct and back beside the watermeadows. The views over the valley are not to be missed, whether southwards towards the Weald and onto the Greensand Ridge

23

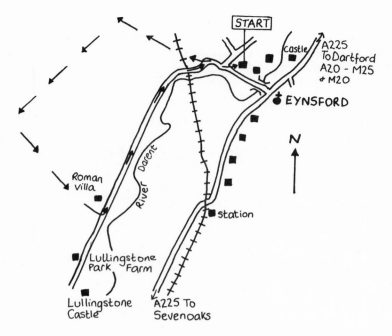

or back over the viaduct to the further slopes of the Downs. Your return to the pub takes you past a Roman villa.

If you extend the walk you can also see Lullingstone Castle. Further on, beside the river, lies the Lullingstone Park Visitors Centre with bookstall, display and tearoom.

The Walk

Turn right as you leave the car park of the Plough and walk up the road, leaving the Darent to your left. If you turn right along Sparepenny Lane you will soon have a good view down to Eynsford Castle, which lies just to your east beside the Darent. For the walk itself, continue past the end of Sparepenny Lane. Leave Darenth Cottage on your right and go towards Hulberry Farm. You get your first view of the viaduct as you follow the road round the bend. The viaduct carries trains from London and Swanley to Sevenoaks and Maidstone.

Almost immediately you will see a large metal gate on the right-hand side of the road with a sign pointing up the field. Go through the narrow entrance to the left of the gate and cross the field on the diagonal towards a stile at the top, where you reach a foot crossing over the railway. Listen for the hooter of any train approaching, cross carefully when you are sure none is coming and go over a stile to the next field. A little further on you get your first full view over the viaduct, back towards Eynsford and over to the Downs.

Continue gently uphill towards a line of trees, go over a stile, cross the farm lane, then take another stile into the next field. From here you can see ahead of you the Greensand Ridge running east-west in the far distance. Halfway across this field you reach an old hedge line. Continue alongside this until you reach another stile. Cross into a lane which forms part of a circular walk around Lullingstone Park and follow the path downhill towards some trees. Pass beside a small stile in the woodland area. Continue down through the wood until you reach some steps onto a road.

To the right lies the path to Lullingstone Castle, $1/2$ mile to the south. About $1/2$ mile beyond Lullingstone Castle is the Lullingstone Park Visitors Centre, which contains some interesting displays of the flora and fauna of the area, as well as a good line in refreshments.

To complete the walk, turn left along the metalled road and walk past the Roman villa. This was discovered in 1949 and dates from between AD 80–90. It is open daily, from 10 am to 4 pm, and gives a remarkable glimpse into the life and lifestyle of a prosperous Roman family. Living room and bath-house walls still stand. This villa held the only Christian chapel known to have existed in a private dwelling in Britain at the time. There are spectacular mosaic tiled floors in the reception rooms.

On leaving the Roman villa, continue along a tarmac road, under the viaduct. The road takes you back to the inn in just under a mile. There is a pleasant tea shop just beyond the ford, where you may buy books of local interest.

Places of interest nearby

Lullingstone Castle is open from April to October, on Saturdays, Sundays and bank holidays, 2 pm to 6 pm. Home-made refreshments are available.

The *Lullingstone Park Visitors Centre* is open daily. Telephone: 01322 865995.

5 Trottiscliffe
The George

Trottiscliffe (pronounced 'Trosley') presents an attractive cluster of oast houses, old barns and weatherboarded cottages on the slopes below the scarp face of the North Downs. The George started as a private dwelling built for a fruit and sheep farmer. It became an alehouse in 1782 and was licensed in 1831. In places you can still see the old beams and peg tiles. There is one open area on two levels, with a fire burning in one of the three fireplaces on cold days. A dining room and a children's room make this a pub for everyone. At the rear is an attractive garden.

You will find a large menu of both regular and special dishes. Starters include soup, prawn cocktail and smoked mackerel. You can have sandwiches and salads, chicken Kiev or lasagne verdi, smoked trout or chicken tikka masala and rice. The puddings are enticing. Fremlins, Wadworth 6X and Old Speckled Hen are on draught, as is a dry cider. Lagers include Heineken and Stella Artois. The times of opening are Monday to Saturday from 11 am to 2.30 pm and 6 pm to 11 pm, Sunday hours are 12 noon to 3 pm and 7 pm to 10.30 pm. Food is always available.

Telephone: 01732 822462.

How to get there: Trottiscliffe lies just north of the eastern end of the M26. Turn south from the M26 at junction 2A. Turn left 200 yards after you join the A25. The George and Dragon is on your left as you enter Trottiscliffe, 1¼ miles north of the A25.

Parking: There is a large car park beside the inn.

Length of the walk: 3 miles. OS maps: Landranger 177 East London area, Pathfinder 1193 Chatham (inn GR 641600).

When the inn was first built the area bore orchards and hop gardens and was known for its sheep rearing. Today the land is mainly arable. The walk takes you through the village, across fields, then traverses part of the scarp face. This is a steep climb but the path is good and the view from the top superb. You continue downhill to an intriguing Neolithic monument, then return to the inn across fields.

The Walk
Turn left as you leave the pub and walk up Taylors Lane. Pass the left turn to Wrotham, then go past a small duck pond. About ¼ mile from the inn turn right into Green Lane. At the end of the road go to the far right-hand corner of the car turning space and take the public bridleway

Converted oast near Trottiscliffe.

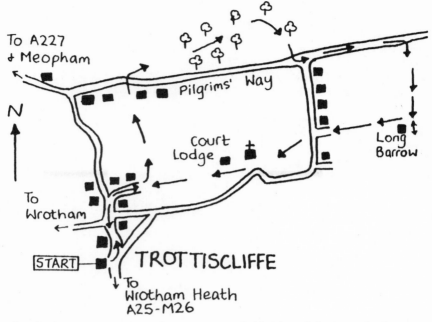

To A227 & Meopham

N

Pilgrims' Way

Court Lodge

Long Barrow

To Wrotham

[START] TROTTISCLIFFE

To Wrotham Heath
A25-M26

ahead, along a narrow track to an open field. Turn left. Pass the houses to your left and head towards the Downs, following the yellow circular walk signs.

When the field opens up to the left you should keep going straight ahead. When you rejoin the hedge line, continue with it on your left. Soon you will reach a narrow path, with a barbed wire fence separating the walker from the grazing. In autumn you will see blackberries and rose hips in the hedgerow. Continue through two kissing gates up to the small road.

This road follows the route known as the Pilgrims' Way which, as popular story goes, is the route taken from Winchester to Canterbury by medieval pilgrims. Cross, go up a few steps, and enter the Trosley Country Park. Turn right along a woodland path, through the frame of a kissing gate, then skirt the road, until the woods open out. Ignore a track which goes down the slope. Take the track straight ahead and start the climb up the chalk.

As you climb, you begin to see the Weald stretching below you. On the slopes there are hazel and guelder rose, typical plants of the chalk downland. At the top you will reach another kissing gate. Pause to take in the view south over the Weald, then go through this and turn right along a well-made track. A woodland seat on the left, where another route goes left, gives you another chance to catch your breath.

To continue, take the route arrowed downward, with a fence on your right-hand side. Go through a gate and continue, with the fence on your left. As you go you will see many old yews, familiar in chalk woodland. Soon the path widens as it drops further, and then brings you out above steep grassland. Follow the arrow straight ahead. This leads you to a stile on your left, marked by a circular '6'. Go through a gate which swings on a weight. Follow the arrow straight ahead, first between trees, then into a wider, steeper stretch. At a small clearing you will find another seat.

Pass an entrance into a field on your right and carry on slightly left, still downhill to the bottom of the scarp. Take the arrow to the right and come out onto the road. Turn left and walk along the Pilgrims' Way. Continue to a whitewashed cottage on your right, then turn right, following the arrow and the National Trust sign to 'Coldrum', and walk down the side of a field. From here you have good views east to the Medway Gap and to the further slopes of the North Downs. At the bottom of the field the path winds slightly to the right, with a few trees arching overhead.

You will find a wide field entrance sloping up to your right. To the left is a marker post with arrows showing different walk routes. Go on for 10 yards until you see some steps leading up to the Coldrum Stones. These are what remains of a communal Neolithic burial site, probably over 4,000 years old.

Return to the wide field entrance, go up the slope to a field, and walk along the south side, with the hedge on your left. Then go ahead and enter a narrow lane between trees. This leads to a small car park. Go along a metalled track for 50 yards to the road. Cross over a stile and follow the fence towards Trottiscliffe church. At the bottom of the field, cross a stile, go down some steps and turn right into another road. The fascinating and complete Norman church of St Peter and St Paul rises to your right.

Pass the church and enter a farmyard. Go past a barn and walk into the field ahead, past an electricity pole bearing a route marker. Cross the field, leaving the fence on your left. At the far side you will reach the bridleway by which you first entered this field at the beginning of the walk. Walk ahead to Taylors Lane. Turn left and walk back ¼ mile to the inn.

Places of interest nearby

The main entrance to the *Trosley Country Park* is signed from the A227 at Vigo.

6 Cobham
The Leather Bottle

Cobham's history goes back to the 13th century when the de Cobhams first acquired the land. The fine church, on an older site, dates from then. In the village street you will see a fascinating range of buildings, some from the 14th century. Later Cobham became a coaching stop on the route from London to Dover.

The Leather Bottle is an impressive, half-timbered inn in the centre of the village. It was built in 1629, in the reign of Charles I, and became a Royalist meeting place in the Civil Wars. Its name stems from the discovery of a leather bottle containing gold sovereigns, hidden in the building. Today it is best known for its connections with Charles Dickens, who lived at Gad's Hill, $3^1/_2$ miles away. Dickens was a frequent visitor to the village and to the inn, and used the setting for parts of *The Pickwick Papers*. The inn is full of paintings, etchings and other Dickens memorabilia. Children are welcome indoors and out, and there is a good play area outside. Every weekend from May to September a garden barbecue is held, with a bouncy castle. There is also in summer a monthly children's entertainer and petanque tournament.

The food (Chef and Brewer, these days) is splendidly reminiscent of Dickens. You could well be lured by Bill Sikes' smokies and

Betsy Trotwood's tomatoes. Tommy Traddles has given his name to trout and even Sairey Gamp leaves an eponymous avocado. There are many more. Children can choose from their own menu. To wash all this down, you could try Webster's Yorkshire Bitter, Wadworth 6X or Theakston XB. Lager drinkers will find Carlsberg, Foster's and Holsten. There is also a wine list. The inn is open from 11 am to 11 pm on weekdays and from 12 noon to 2.30 pm and 7 pm to 10.30 pm on Sundays. Bar food is available throughout the day on weekdays and from 12 noon to 2.30 pm and from 7 pm to 9.30 pm on Sundays. The restaurant is open from 12 noon to 2.30 pm and from 7 pm to 9.30 pm every day except Sunday evenings.
Telephone: 01474 814327.

How to get there: To reach Cobham leave the M25 at junction 2 or come off the M2 west of the Medway bridge at Rochester at junction 1. Take the B2009 south from the A2, 5 miles west of the Medway bridge. The Leather Bottle is a mile from here, opposite the church.

Parking: There is a parking area beside the pub.

Length of the walk: 3 miles. OS maps: Landranger 177 East London area, Pathfinder 1193 Chatham (inn GR 670686).

The walk sets out past the 13th-century church of St Mary Magdalene and Cobham College and takes you across downland fields to the slopes near Henley Street. It then leads you along the top of fields from where you can see over to the beautiful slopes beyond Luddesdown. You skirt Cobhambury wood and return along the edge of historic Cobham Park. There is a chance to enjoy the flowers and trees of the chalk downland as well as savour the history of this attractive village. Nearby is Owletts, a small 17th-century house owned by the National Trust.

The Walk

Turn left at the inn door. Before you cross the road to the churchyard steps, you will see the small sarsen stone, with its incomprehensible words, at the corner of the building. This is a survivor from many lumps of sandstone collected by Bronze Age men and used for a megalith. Other sarsen stones were incorporated into the church walls. Among the interesting features in the church of St Mary Magdalene you will see a fine chancel and an outstanding collection of medieval brasses. Now walk on round the right, west, side of the church past the entrance to Cobham College. Later an almshouse and now providing sheltered accommodation, Cobham College was originally a college for five priests who prayed for the souls of the de Cobham family.

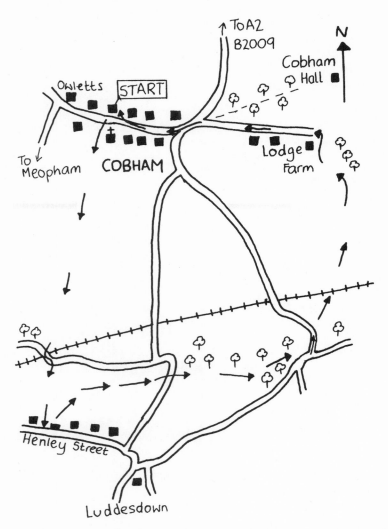

Take the path straight ahead. This leads beside an extension to the churchyard to a stile leading onto a broad, open field. Immediately, you get your first impressions of the great sweep of the downland ahead, towards and beyond Luddesdown. To the east you can see the continuation of the North Downs beyond the Medway. Walk down this field, past an orchard. The field curves slightly to the right as you reach the bottom. On your way you will pass tall standard beeches, sweet chestnut, elder, oak and hazel. Leave the field and go on for about

30 yards to the lane. Turn left and cross the railway. This carries the line from London to Dover.

Proceed for about 70 yards, then turn right just before a white house, along the public footpath, leaving the garden hedge on your left. At the end of the field take a few paces between thick bushes to a stile. Follow the footpath across a short field to a kissing gate, then walk down the next field towards Henley Street. At the bottom you will see a narrow lane leading between gardens, down to a road. Ignore this and double back at 45° to follow the path, signed to 'Cobhambury Wood'.

At the top right-hand corner of the field turn right and cross into the next field to the east, following the sign for 'footpath 189'. Walk along the top, northern, side of the field, with the hedge on your left. You will see much of the guelder rose, with its white flower in spring or its dark, almost black, fruit in autumn. Cherry trees also flourish in the hedgerow. You will also see how flinty and thin the top soil is. Then, looking further afield, you will see again the slopes to the south beyond Luddesdown. At end of this field pass the sign directing walkers to 'Batts Road'. This would take you to a road leading back to Cobham, but it is worth going on past Cobhambury Wood.

To do this, continue to the field entrance and turn left up a narrow lane. Walk on for 30 yards, then turn right, following the 'Camer Park circular walk' sign. This takes you below Cobhambury Wood, between hedges, and gives you the best glimpses of all of the Luddesdown valley. The woods to your left are dense, old coppice woodland. You can also see here the way an old coppice hedge grows up from its 'stool'.

The path begins to drop down and then, as you reach the power line, to curve left. Pass the stile which leads back into a field on the Camer Park circular walk. This is the most southerly point of Cobhambury Wood. The space to either side now widens and you begin to see conifers on your right. Just 20 yards ahead turn right into woodland along a wide track, between coppiced hazel, and continue downhill. As the track levels out you reach the road, emerging from the woods under a metal bar at a three-way junction.

Turn left. You will now see two railway bridges ahead. Turn up the rough track and make for the bridge on the right-hand side. Walk up this track for ½ mile. At the top you will come to a collection of farm cottages and buildings. At the T-junction you will see Cobham Park and Cobham Hall ahead. Cobham Hall, now a girls' school, was originally the home of the Cobhams, Brookes and then the Darnleys. The building, open occasionally through the year, spans several centuries and is well worth visiting. Turn left and walk for another ½ mile along the lane to the war memorial at the beginning of Cobham village, beside the entrance drive to Cobham Park. Go ahead into Cobham village, past the Ship inn and several weatherboarded cottages. The Darnley Arms,

Sarsen stone.

the oldest inn in Cobham, is said to have been linked to the college to enable the monks to slip over when they felt the need. Here, young readers of Penelope Lively will also enjoy the tale told on the wall of the real ghost of Thomas Kemp.

Immediately after the next block of buildings you return to the Leather Bottle.

7 Shorne
The Rose and Crown

The earliest part of the Rose and Crown, in the centre of Shorne village, was built in the reign of Henry VIII and became an alehouse in the 18th century. First known as Ye Olde Billett, then the Crooked Billett, its name was changed to the Rose and Crown in 1812. Today the two bars are in the original private house. The restaurant was once the old bakery next door. Beside an inglenook fireplace is a tiny cupboard in which a baby could sleep in warmth. Children are welcome and are given their own crayoning book.

Excellent, home-made food with variety – and plenty of it – is the hallmark here. Mixed grills, steak and kidney pudding, even liver and bacon are available, as well as interesting bar food. A roast meal is served on Sundays and children's portions are available. In addition to the usual range of drinks you will find Ruddles County and Ruddles Best, Webster's Yorkshire, and Courage Best. The Rose and Crown is open from 11 am to 2.30 pm and 6 pm to 11 pm from Monday to Saturday. On Sundays it opens from 12 noon to 3 pm and from 7 pm to 10.30 pm.

Telephone: 01474 822373.

View near Shorne of St Mary's church, Chalk.

How to get there: Shorne is just south of the A226 Gravesend to Rochester road. The turning is signposted 1¼ miles east of Chalk church. The Rose and Crown is ½ mile from the A226, at a sharp turn in the road.

Parking: You can park beside the inn.

Length of the walk: 2 miles. OS maps: Landranger 177 East London area, Pathfinder 1177 Gravesend and Tilbury (inn GR 691711).

Shorne, on the northern edge of the Downs, takes its name from the Saxon word 'scora' which means a steep slope. There are plenty of these on this interesting walk – and consequently lots of good views. From Shorne Hill you look over arable fields, then over the Shorne and Higham marshes, towards the Lower Hope reach of the Thames. You walk along a lower slope and see the chestnuts of Randall Wood on the skyline above, then return past remnants of ancient woodland, along a track centuries old.

The Walk
Turn left as you leave the inn and walk up Butchers Hill, leaving the entrance to the interesting church of St Peter and St Paul on your left.

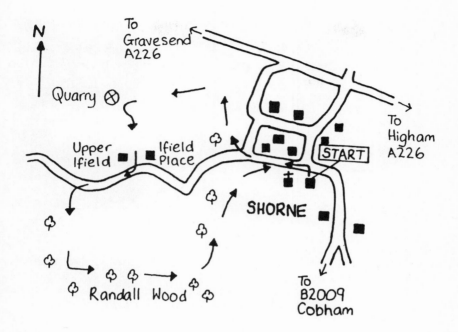

Go up a tarmac path between two metal posts. At the top you will see a second pair of posts, leading onto a gravelled entrance with a half-timbered thatched house on your right. Follow the path between the houses until you reach the road. Ahead you will see a small thicket of young elms which have grown out of the suckers from trees that succumbed to the Dutch elm disease in the 1970s.

Turn right, leaving a garage with a double pitched roof on the right-hand corner. Almost immediately, cross the road to a small parking area. Ahead you will see a swing, climbing frame and chute plus two seats. Follow the yellow, arrowed, circular walk sign diagonally across the green to a marker post bearing another arrow. Follow the signed path under spreading oak trees into a wooded area where steps are set into the path. These lead you to Shorne Hill, nearly 300 feet above sea level.

To continue, turn left before you reach the top. Cross a tall stile, take a narrow path through a small shaw, and go down five steps to the edge of a field.

From here you can take in still more views, showing some of the rich texture of Thameside, past and present. In the near distance you can see, marked by the small tower of St Mary's church, the village of Chalk. Here Charles Dickens spent his honeymoon, and several holidays afterwards. Still on the south side of the Thames, you will see Gravesend

37

and the white spire of St George's church, where the Princess Pocahontas is buried.

Turn right and follow the yellow arrow on a post tucked into the hedge. A good, well-trodden path runs along the narrow headland. Go down to the hedge line at the bottom of the field. The path then swings to the right and you make your way towards yellow markers painted on a concrete block. Turn left and walk down a sunken track between holly and beech.

The hedge ends just as you come to another set of yellow arrows. Keep going straight ahead, following the path, first above the bank, then below it. Cross a stile carved with the 'Shorne Park circular walk' legend. Go slightly left, then straight across the field to the edge of a disused quarry. Turn left at the quarry along a cart track. At first you will see an old barn and two cowl-less oasts ahead of you. Follow the path between two houses and turn right onto the road at Ifield Place. Go past a converted, weatherboarded house and pass woodland beside you on the left. After ½ mile the road swings to the right. Here, opposite a telegraph pole, the familiar yellow marker leads you left from the road. Go up a sunken, tree-lined lane. You will notice the trees getting taller, and the roots of the beeches spreading over the bank above you. At the top you come to more signs. To the right lies the way into the Shorne Country Park.

Turn left to return to Shorne and follow a path, centuries old, between the trees. To your left you see the fields dropping back down to the Thames. To your right stretch the coppiced chestnuts of Randall Wood, first introduced to provide hop poles. In places you will see fascinating formations where entire new trunks have grown out of the coppiced 'stool'.

Cross a small culvert, then climb up again along an easy, pleasant and shady path. Go up some steps set into the hillside. Wind round past more coppiced chestnut. Continue along some level ground, then up some more steps. Watch for odd stumps or roots.

You will reach a stile leading into a meadow on your right. Turn left at this point. Follow a marker post, pointing ahead, to a broad, open area. You now continue along a gravel path, then a wide, grassy track. This leads you on into a narrower path, past marker posts, to a double stile leading onto Mill Hill Lane. Soon you see again the open space and the doubled pitched garage roof where you first emerged from Butchers Hill.

Turn right and go down Butchers Hill back to the inn.

Places of interest nearby
Shorne Country Park, with visitors centre and refreshments, is open from 8 am to sunset, daily. It is approached from the B2009 south of Shorne.

8 Cliffe
The Black Bull

Once the people of Cliffe provided a ship for the protection of the realm. Then the waterways silted up and marshland encroached. Now the small town stands on the edge of Thames marshland. The fine church, St Helen's, indicates Cliffe's importance in the Middle Ages. The Black Bull stands on the corner nearest the marsh, a solid Victorian pub, with great warmth and vitality within and a Roman well downstairs. Children are welcome in a room beside the bar area, as well as in the Tapestries restaurant.

The Black Bull offers one of the widest ranges of real ales imaginable, as well as all the usual drinks. Names like Arthur Pendragon and Thomas Hardy Country Strong Bitter take their turn with Tsing Tao and San Miguel. Its Malaysian, Indonesian and Chinese cuisine has acquired a well-deserved reputation. Set meals and à la carte dishes from a wide selection are available – aromatic duck or orange chicken, and seasonable vegetables in oyster sauce are only a few from the long list. The bar is open from 12 noon until 3 pm, and 7 pm to 11 pm, Mondays to Saturdays. Sundays 12 noon to 3 pm and 7 pm to 10.30 pm. The restaurant is open from 7 pm to 10 pm, each evening except Sunday and Monday.

Telephone: 01634 220893.

How to get there: Cliffe is 7 miles from Gravesend and 7 from Chatham, at the end of the B2000 from Strood. Turn sharp right into Reed Street when you see the Black Bull on the near right-hand corner.

Parking: You can park beside the inn, in Reed Street.

Length of the walk: 3½ miles. OS maps: Landranger 178 The Thames Estuary, Pathfinder 1177 Gravesend and Tilbury (inn GR 737766).

The Thames marshes of the Hoo peninsula have a special appeal. There is a timeless feel here, although until the Middle Ages the marshland had not fully encroached. In winter the wide skies fill with migrant birds. The remote feeling is best epitomised by Charles Dickens' account of Pip's meeting with the convict, Magwitch, in 'Great Expectations'. This walk takes you across fields with views of that marshland towards the estuary. It also takes you to Pip's meeting place. You will also pass Cooling Castle, once home of the de Cobhams.

The Walk

Turn right out of the pub and walk along Reed Street until you see the de-restriction sign. Turn right into Thatchers Lane just before the sign. Go to the top, turn right, then immediately left at a marker showing the circular route sign. Walk along a concrete track that leads into a broad, open field track at a public footpath sign. Follow the path signed diagonally left, for 500 yards across the field, or go ahead to the second of two power posts, then turn left to meet the hedge 350 yards on.

This area is rich arable land. The rectangular shape of the fields dates from Roman days. On your left the marshland extends northwards. Beyond the marsh you see, across the Thames, the cooling towers of Canvey Island in Essex. At the hedge turn right and walk beside it to the Cooling road. Walk carefully ahead, south, for 100 yards to the next corner, then follow the public footpath sign, left across the field, towards Berry Court Farm. Go along the old hedge line, if you prefer, if the path has not been re-instated after ploughing. At the far side of the field you will see the name 'Merryboys Riding School' on the gable-end of the granary facing you.

Turn right. About 100 yards ahead turn left, over a stile, into a paddock and head for a stile on the far side, centre. The trodden path takes you round the field, starting with the hedge on your left side. Cross the stile, then head diagonally right to do a (walking) hurdle course over four stiles. The second and third of these take you across a short, sandy gallop belonging to the riding school, so check carefully to make sure it is not about to be used.

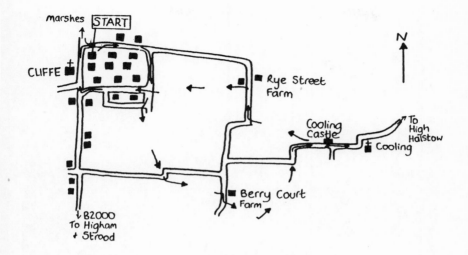

You will see a yellow marker post in the last field. Make for this, then turn at about 90° left and make for another stile further up the fence line. Cross this, then go over one more stile, diagonally right, ahead of you. You should now be able to see a tall post at 45° ahead right, at the end of a narrow line of low trees. Make for this, or skirt the headlands if you prefer. From here you will now have a clear view of Cooling Castle, and St James' church at Cooling.

When you reach the marker post walk along the hedge line to the road. Walk up the road, then turn right until you reach a 30 mph limitation sign just before a low stone bridge. Walk on now past Cooling Castle where in 1381 John de Cobham fortified his manor house against possible raids from the estuary by the French.

In the churchyard of St James, 300 yards beyond, you may now imagine the mists which swirled up from the marsh when young Pip visited his family's graves. 'Pip's Graves' are there, tombs of children who may have died from malaria.

Now return along the road to the low stone bridge, where you will see a public footpath sign taking you diagonally across a field to a stile. You will notice the red helmet, sign of the Saxon Shore Way. This long distance path runs along the coast from Gravesend to Rye and includes the line of fortifications built by the Romans as defences against Saxon raiders. Follow the sign across the field, cross a stile then go to a point in the middle of some willows just south of a gate in the far corner. Cross a small bridge to the right of the sixth willow down. Turn diagonally left, then follow the hedge line along the side of the field to a stile in the

St Helen's church.

corner. The next field slopes up here and you should be able to make out, at 45° to your right, a fingerpost ahead where a road runs. Make for this across the field, or follow the headland round, right, to the road.

Turn right from the fingerpost. Opposite Rye Street Farm take the path across the field. Halfway across you will meet an old hedge line, which marks a division between higher old land and land sloping down to marshes. Continue in a straight line until you emerge into Thatchers Lane opposite Swingate Road. Return to the centre of Cliffe along this road. Turn right at the end of Swingate Road and return along the main street of Cliffe to the Black Bull.

9 Boxley
The King's Arms

The small village of Boxley has long welcomed people as they pass on
their way up and down the beautiful Boxley valley. The King's Arms has
been at the centre of this tradition for 900 years. In the early days monks
from the nearby abbey brewed ale here and distributed it to pilgrims and
travellers. Later, the place became a coaching house. The name refers
to the coat of arms of Richard II, who came to Boxley in 1381. By
this time the house was already 200 years old. Today, you can still see
vestiges of the early single farm building, which would have been a hall
open to the roof with a fire burning in the centre of the floor. Now,
however, the old timbers have mellowed, the fire burns in the inglenook
and you will find prints and photographs on the walls.

The well-cooked food includes a carvery roast on Sundays. Special
meals of the day range from rabbit stew and dumplings to pasta spirale
cooked in red wine with tuna, tomato and mushroom bake or Chinese
chicken stir fry. There is a choice of 'Old English' pies and a wide range
of vegetarian dishes. The children's menu offers chips, baked beans,
chicken nuggets and other favourites. As for drinks, the proprietors
cater for a wide range of tastes. The choice of real ales is extensive and
it varies. At one time you might find Fuller's London Pride, Wadworth

6X and Boddingtons Bitter, at another Abbot Ale, Brakspear beers, Flowers IPA and Fremlins. There is a small beer festival three or four times a year, to see what people want, and plenty of flexibility. Wines and champagnes, including non-alcoholic drinks, are also available. This is a friendly place, where both visitors and local people feel at home. Children can join you in the dining areas and there is a large garden at the back, where they can play. Dogs are also welcome.

The King's Arms is open daily from 11 am to 11 pm on Monday to Saturday. On Sunday the opening times are from 12 noon to 3 pm and 7 pm to 10.30 pm. Food is served from 12 noon to 2 pm and 7 pm to 9 pm.

Telephone: 01622 755177.

How to get there: Leave the M20 at junction 7 and take the A249 to Maidstone. Turn right to Penenden Heath and Sandling. At a roundabout beside a green, turn right to Boxley. Boxley village is 1 mile ahead.

Parking: You can park in the elongated square opposite the pub, in front of the church.

Length of the walk: 3 miles. OS maps: Landranger 188 Maidstone and The Weald of Kent, Pathfinder 1209 Maidstone (inn GR 774590).

This walk takes you past the medieval church of St Mary and All Saints, across field paths in historic parkland and up the scarp face of the North Downs. From there the walk follows the North Downs Way for a while before dropping down to the valley and returning between fields and traditional orchards, along the remains of what may well be an old Roman road.

The Walk

On leaving the King's Arms cross the road and walk towards the lychgate of the church. This is well-worth visiting, with many features of interest. You will see dogtooth decoration on the top of one of two exposed capitals in the north wall of the large entrance. Once inside the body of the church, note the pillars of the nave, which lean outwards to resemble a boat, 'the ark of God'.

To pursue the walk, look for a stile which stands a few paces north of the lychgate. Cross and take the path which runs diagonally up the field, following the fence line on your left. Turn left after the next stile and make your way to another stile beside a narrow road. This is part of the route known as the Pilgrims' Way, which runs between Winchester and Canterbury.

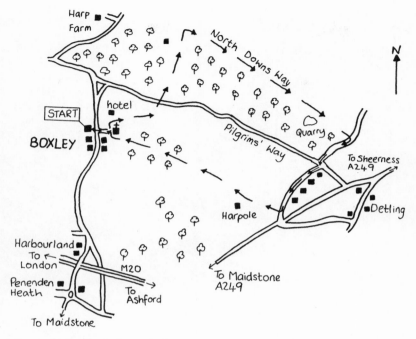

Cross both the stile and the road, then enter a narrow lane between a hedge on your left and a fence on your right. Continue up the hill, which rises more steeply now, to the top of the field on the right. Pass a stile which bears an arrow pointing ahead and continue uphill to the top. On your way up you will see a deep, heavily-wooded combe dropping down to your right.

This is a fairly steep climb, rising over 250 ft in 1/3 mile. Once you reach a kissing gate at the top your effort will be more than rewarded by the view. The rest of the walk is either downhill or on the level.

Turn right. The broad track along which you now find yourself walking is part of the North Downs Way, from where, between the trees, you have occasional glimpses of the Weald below and the Greensand Ridge beyond. Continue along the track for just over a mile. At one point you skirt an old chalk quarry below you on your right. At the end you step over a low barrier, then turn right along a narrow path and start to make your way downhill. Ignore the route markers you see leading through a gate ahead, and follow the main, stony path further downhill, as it bends to the right.

As you continue down the main track the old chalk quarry shows more clearly to your right, well overgrown with rowan and beech. Further down still, the path becomes sunken, with old yews whose roots

St Mary and All Saints.

you can see on the banks. You now pass a working quarry to your left and continue along a concrete track to the Pilgrims' Way. Turn left, then right, down Harples Lane. After ¼ mile you will see a house with hung tiles and with a well in the garden. Turn right immediately after it and make your way along a broad farm track. To the right, across a field, you can see up to where you have just walked along the Downs.

Go past Harpole Farm, passing a triangular stand of trees to your left, then continue ahead, and leave a large barn to your right. At the end of the next field the track curves slightly to the left and continues between trees. Soon you will see a yellow arrow pointing you straight on, stuck onto an old shed on your right. At the end of the hedge line you come to a cherry orchard on your left, with standard fruit trees, beneath which, in traditional style, sheep often graze. Beyond the orchard the main track swings to the left. At this point you will see a wooden gate on your right. Cross the stile into a field and go straight ahead, alongside a barbed wire fence on your left. Cross a stile and walk beside a fence, with hawthorn on your left.

Come to another stile, with a number of rowans and a very large, old beech on your right in the fence. After the stile at this fence, follow the path under some huge chestnut trees to the corner of the churchyard wall. Go under two spreading beeches and continue to the stile at which you began the walk. Cross and walk across the square to the inn.

10 Ulcombe
The Pepper Box

Once the Horseshoe, this delightful pub in open country at Fairborne Heath at Ulcombe, has long been known as the Pepper Box, taking its name from an early type of pistol. You can see it represented on the unusual inn sign outside. The Pepper Box used to be yet another haunt for smugglers. In this case, it provided a stopping place on the route inland from the Romney Marsh. Inside, the inn is very well furnished and comfortable, with an inglenook fireplace and well-spaced small tables. There is a separate dining room where families are welcome. Outside is a pleasant, secluded garden.

The food is excellent, with fish, brought fresh daily from Dungeness, a speciality. The regular menu, always available, offers a wide range of starters. Main courses include home-made fish pie and steak and kidney pudding. Plaice belamar and sole bonne femme are among the many fish dishes. There are also splendid 'specials', which change every two to three days. Children's portions are served if requested. Shepherd Neame Master Brew and Bishops Finger are supplied on draught. You will also find Hürlimann's and Steinbok lagers and Dry Blackthorn cider. Home-made wines are available by the glass.

The times of opening are from 11 am to 3 pm and 6.30 pm to 11 pm

on weekdays, 12 noon to 2.30 pm and 7 pm to 10.30 pm on Sundays.
Telephone: 01622 842558.

How to get there: From the A20 take the B2163 south towards Leeds
and Langley, then the A274 to Sutton Valence, then Headcorn. Turn left
towards Ulcombe, then right after 3 miles, at a triangle. The Pepper Box
is ⅝ mile ahead. Alternatively, turn south to Ulcombe from the turning
off the A20 just to the west of the point where the M20 flies over. Take
the first left after 1½ miles, then first right at the triangle. The Pepper
Box is well signed.

Parking: You can park beside the inn.

Length of the walk: 2¾ miles. OS maps: Landranger 189 Ashford and
Romney Marsh area, Pathfinders 1210 Harrietsham and 1230 Headcorn
and Charing (inn GR 858501).

*Time seems to have stood still in this part of Kent. You walk across open
fields, through coppiced woodland, old nutteries and apple orchards, then
return through combes and over small rises on the edge of the Greensand
Ridge. Here, still more orchards spread out below you. On a clear day
you can see Dungeness, beyond the Romney Marsh, Fairlight near
Hastings and even to Quarry Hill near Southborough. You can follow
the Greensand Way down to Ulcombe's interesting church, if you wish.*

The Walk
Turn left as you leave the Pepper Box and walk down the road for ⅛ mile
to a stile set into the hedge on the left-hand side. The post bears the sign
of the Greensand Way. Cross into a broad field and walk towards the
corner of a hedge straight ahead of you. Here you will see a post, set back
into the hedge, again showing the Greensand Way sign. Cut through the
gap and walk along the headland of the adjacent field, with the hedge line
on your left. This is privet with pollarded poplars rising above it, planted
to serve as a windbreak.
    At the end of the windbreak cross the short gap, where the plough
turns into the left-hand field. Go through the hedge, cross a lane and
enter the field ahead. The footpath cuts diagonally left across the field
to the end of a line of poplars. Either follow this line or walk straight
ahead along the headland, leaving the hedge on your right. If you do the
latter, turn left at the far right-hand corner of the field, then go on to a
gate in the fence which is level with the end of the poplars.
    Cross the stile and enter some old hazel coppice. Cross another stile at
the end. Take a slight left turn, then a right turn as you continue through
the coppice. At the next stile you enter an apple orchard. Leave the main

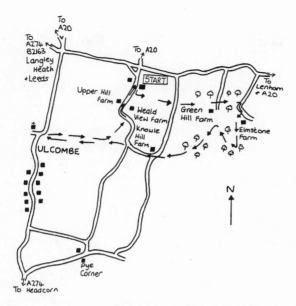

track as it swings to the right and cross the stile ahead. Follow the hedge line on the right to the far corner of the orchard. Here you will find an exceptionally tall stile set into the corner.

Cross the stile, then double back along the narrow road and follow it down as far as Elmstone Farm. You will see an old oast on your left just opposite the wide entrance. Turn right and follow the tarmac drive to a gateway ahead, where the house drive swings left.

Go through the gate and continue along a grassy track beside a small culvert. Bend right and cross into a field which slopes gently upwards ahead of you. As you cross you will see, ahead and slightly below you on your left, one of the many 'tanks' found along the Greensand Way. These ponds have been made where water emerges along the spring line. Behind your left shoulder stands the church of Boughton Malherbe on the skyline. The whole area below makes a wonderful sight, especially when apple blossom is in flower. Follow the posts across the field to a hedge with woodland beyond, where you will see a sign reading 'Footpath this way'. Cross the stile into the woods and follow a clear path, which winds its way through to another field.

Walk up the slope, with woodland on your right. Turn right into the woods, where you see a yellow arrow under an ash tree, then wind upwards along the top of a wooded ridge. Take care here as you will have something of a scramble. As you emerge from the woodland, you will find yourself at the south-eastern corner of a field. Ahead lies Green Hill Farm. The right of way leads you ahead and back across the field but

All Saints' church.

it is normal here simply to turn left and walk straight along the headland to the south-western, left-hand, corner of the field.

Here you will see a post with a yellow arrow set back into the hedge line, between old coppiced beech. Go through the gap and pick up a farm track which leads between fruit bushes, then into an open field. Leave a large metal barn on your left as you follow the track round a curve. Soon after this another track rises up the slope below you to join you on the left. Here, too, you will have amazing views south. Now go straight ahead along the farm track, between hedges. At the end of the track follow the road straight ahead past Knowle Hill.

At the T-junction follow the footpath ahead and go down the hillside, taking care in wet weather because of the drop immediately on your right. You will soon reach a low stile. Cross this and walk alongside a fence until the path curves to the left. Just after the turning you will see, in the hedge on the right, a stile with a yellow marker and the Greensand Way sign. The stile looks elderly but is perfectly sound, so climb over it into a field.

At this point you have the choice of walking on to Ulcombe church, or of completing the circular walk. To return to the pub, go right and walk up the side of the field, with the hedge on your right. Make for a stile at the top. This takes you into an old nuttery. Walk up the side, with the hedge on your left, to another stile. This requires a good leg up as it straddles an unexpected slope, but once over this you are on the road, just below Upper Hill Farm. Turn left and follow the road back to the Pepper Box.

To visit Ulcombe church, or just look at it from above, walk on from the stile marked with the Greensand Way sign. Cross the field taking a diagonal path slightly to the left towards the far left-hand corner, pausing to look at the splendid views to the south-west. In the far corner the Greensand Way arrow on the stile takes you left, then right, along the southern headland of the next field. Follow the line of poplars to their end and look ahead to the tower of Ulcombe church nestling in the trees. A marker bearing yellow arrows leads you straight ahead and down into the valley. According to legend, William the Conqueror stood on the site of the church and gave orders for it to be built. You will find a host of interesting features, including some good monumental brasses and two medieval wall paintings. Outside, the yew tree in the churchyard is said to be 3,000 years old. Retrace your steps to complete the walk.

11 Tenterden
The William Caxton

Tenterden grew up from Saxon times as the 'den' or pig pasture of the people from Thanet. In the Middle Ages it became an important market centre for the area. Today, the spacious High Street is lined with Tudor, Georgian and Victorian houses. Tenterden is also the terminus of the Kent and East Sussex Light Railway.

The William Caxton, named in honour of the first English printer, who grew up nearby, stands at West Cross, some 400 yards from the centre. Dating from the 16th century, as the old beams and the fireplace suggest, it has a small restaurant at one end and a cosy, traditional atmosphere, helped by hop bines and old prints, throughout. There is a small beer garden at the back. The home-made food is ideal. From the bacon roll in the bar menu to the chef's own skate or the apple crumble, all is delicious. The children's menu could not be wider. The inn is owned by Shepherd Neame. You will find their own Master Brew, Best Bitter, Spitfire and Bishops Finger on draught, as is Hürlimann's lager. The selection of wines is good and wide-ranging.

The William Caxton is open on Monday to Friday from 11 am to 3 pm and 5 pm to 11 pm, all day on Saturday, and on Sunday from 12 noon to 3 pm and 7 pm to 10.30 pm. Food is served at all times, except Sunday evening.

Telephone: 01580 763142.

How to get there: The William Caxton is at the junction of the A28 Hastings road and the B2082 Rye road.

Parking: There is limited parking in front of the inn, also on the B2082. Otherwise head for a town car park, such as the one beside the museum in Station Road or the station car park.

Length of the walk: 3 miles. OS maps: Landranger 189 Ashford and Romney Marsh area, Pathfinder 1250 Tenterden (inn GR 879331).

This walk takes you into the Weald, immediately to the north of Tenterden. You cross the railway line, then meander across fields, up and down gentle slopes to a point from which you can see over to the South Downs. You return towards Tenterden, with the magnificent church of St Mildred always on the skyline. On all these slopes you will see descendants of the sheep who gave Tenterden its fortune when, from the 14th to the 17th century, the town flourished at the centre of the Wealden manufacture of broadcloth. The woods and shaws are what remains of the dense woodland cleared first for grazing, then for export and for ship-building at the one-time port of Smallhythe, 2 miles away. The railway station and the museum come at the end.

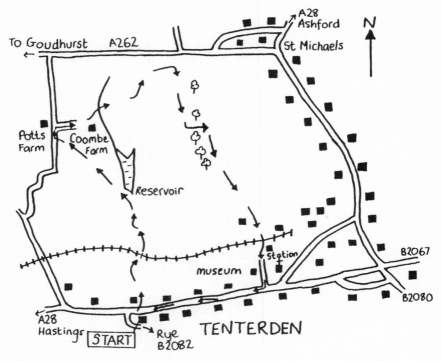

The Walk

Cross the A28 to West Cross Gardens and walk to the far left-hand side of the close. Go along a track, first metalled then grassy, to a stile, set diagonally ahead of you. Cross and follow the path downhill towards some oak trees. You will see the tower of St Mildred's church on your right. Follow the beeches on the fence line, down the slope to another stile, then continue to the railway. Stopping, looking and listening before crossing is no hardship when you may be rewarded by the sight of a 'P' class or the Manning Wardle 'Charwelton' approaching. Then cross the field beyond the railway, with the hedge beside you on your right.

Go over a stile at the bottom of this field, then take the path which crosses the next field at 45°, to the corner of a shaw. This extends into the field from the right. Skirt the trees, then go ahead to an opening into the next field beside an oak. Cross a narrow field towards a metal gate. Climb over the somewhat steep stile beside the gate and go ahead, downhill, following the arrow reading 'AB 20'. Negotiate the fallen tree which serves, ingeniously, as a stile. Cross the footbridge over a small stream, then go up the slope towards a stunted oak. Follow the clearly trodden path on and down, left, to cross a patch of ground where the path is made easier by old sleepers laid crosswise.

Walk up the next slope, under a gnarled beech and past two tree stumps on your right. Go ahead between oaks, towards the corner of a garden. Make for a swing-gate beside the fence, then follow a stone wall up to a hedge. Cross a stile, and turn right onto the road.

After 100 yards you will see an arrow pointing right, in the shape of a fish. Follow this into the driveway to Coombe Farm and Tenterden Trout Waters. Go down a concrete track between fences until you reach a crossing of four tracks. There is a small pond ahead, on your right. Cross the stile at the corner of the field on your left-hand side and follow the public footpath, signed to 'St Michaels'.

You will see a yellow marker post on the further corner of a low, long shed. Go past this and walk down the slope to a stile set in a thick hedge. Cross the stile to a bridge with single plank over a small stream, ducking carefully under the overhanging branches. Follow the right of way, left, at 45° up the next slope or turn left, then right, along and up the headland. Turn left through a wide opening and skirt the fence line, leaving a pond and a small shaw on your right. As the trees end, you will come to a stile over a new barbed wire fence. Cross this and head for the far, top, right-hand corner of the field. You will see farm buildings at the top to guide you and a tall tree beside a gateway.

You will be rewarded by a sight of the South Downs near Fairlight and Hastings. Now double back down the field, leaving the eastern hedge on your left. You will find an elderly but efficient stile set into the hedge, almost opposite the stile by which you first entered. Cross the eastern stile, turn right and continue your walk downhill, this time leaving fence, trees and a narrow ghyll on your right.

Pass a pond on your left. Skirt a stile and go through a small shaw of mixed coppice and standards to the next field. You will now see St Mildred's clearly ahead. The tower with its splendid pinnacles was built in the 15th century, at the height of Tenterden's wealth. Walk across a potentially muddy area, made passable by two lines of railway sleepers. Go over another stile, then continue straight ahead.

Go through some more old coppice, leaving a pond on your left, and enter the next field. At the next stile you will see people fishing below to your right. Head to the left towards the second of two power posts. As you come to the top of the slope you will see a yellow-topped marker post. Make for this and cross the stile. Now go more steeply downhill, following the path to the right of the next power post. Go down some steps and over a clapper stile, cross a small bridge and continue ahead up the field. Go under the overhead cable, aiming a degree to the right of St Mildred's church. In this field you may encounter a temporary metal stile on an electric fence. Go through it and continue up the field, beside the hedge on your right, to another clapper gate. Cross the station car park and go over the level crossing.

Steam engine at the Kent and East Sussex Light Railway.

The entrance to the station is on your left. It is an important place for all lovers of steam engines. The railway houses 16, 6 of which are in working use. Trains run all year round on the round trip to Northiam and back. There is a station bookshop for enthusiasts of all ages.

Go straight up the road ahead. On your left is the Whistle Stop café, open all day. You will see the museum and car park on your right. The museum (telephone: 01580 764310) contains an excellent account of Tenterden's history and shows how the town flourished as one of the Cinque Ports until the port at Smallhythe silted up.

Turn right into the main road and make your way back to the inn, 350 yards ahead on the left.

12 Cranbrook
The Windmill Inn

Like Tenterden, Cranbrook was from the late Middle Ages an important centre for the weaving of broadcloth. You can see many houses still standing, from the prosperous times of the 15th and 16th centuries. Visible from most corners is the large, 18th-century smock mill, still in working order.

The Windmill Inn stands on the slope above the centre of the town, set back from the road. It is a friendly place, in traditional style, with photographs of old Cranbrook on the walls. The home-made and well-cooked meals include chicken, fish and steak. A pleasant, small dining room with oak settles makes a good place to take children. A log fire burns when it is cold and, in summer, there are Sunday barbecues and cream teas. The draught ales are from Shepherd Neame—Master Brew, Bishops Finger and Spitfire. You will also find Swan Light ale and Whitbread White Label, and a good range of lagers and wines.

The pub is open all day from 11 am to 11 pm Mondays to Saturdays in summer, from 11 am to 3 pm and 6 pm to 11 pm in winter. Sundays throughout the year from 12 noon to 3 pm and 7 pm to 10.30 pm.

Telephone: 01580 713119.

Church of St Dunstan.

How to get there: Take the A229 south from the junction with the A262, then go left on the B2189 after ¼ mile. The Windmill is ½ mile ahead on the right.

Parking: You can park beside and in front of the inn.

Length of the walk: 2¾ miles. OS maps: Landranger 188 Maidstone and The Weald of Kent, Pathfinder 1249 Wadhurst, Cranbrook and Bewl Bridge Reservoir (inn GR 778366).

To start this walk you take a path across a playing field towards the church, then return to the road to cross and walk along a clear track to woodland. Hops were grown for several centuries here. There were also ironworks in the area. Now you see sheep grazing again. You go through small stretches of woodland and return beside some land currently set aside from farming.

The Walk
Go down the narrow lane flanked by hedges, just to the south of the Windmill. Cross the field to the far corner. Children will enjoy the swings and long horse set to one side there. You will see the windmill rising over the roof tops to the south-east. The sandstone church of

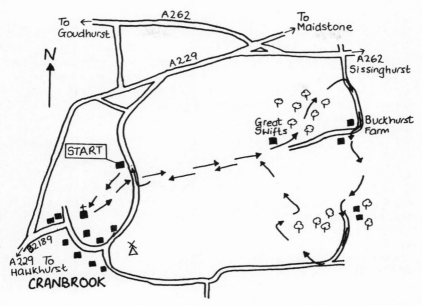

St Dunstan, ahead, is another prominent feature in the town. Inside are two fonts, one constructed in 1725 for total immersion but, it is said, used only twice.

Turn back along the lower hedge line and go ahead to the road. Go down the steps to the pavement, cross the road and take the public footpath opposite, signed to 'Sissinghurst'. Walk on, with open fields on your right and the neat lawns of Great Swifts on your left. At the end of this garden cross a stile into the continuation of the lane. Continue to a concrete farm road and follow this until it bends to the right. At this point go along the hedge line on the left to a stile. Follow the path into woods and go downhill to a field. Now walk up the field to another stile. Take care here as the lower step on the further side of the stile is a long way down and there are steps beyond, leading down to a narrow road. The path to Sissinghurst village continues straight ahead for ½ mile.

For the circular walk, turn right and walk down to Buckhurst Farm. Go over a stile beside a large metal gate into the farmyard. Opposite the stables, just before the house, turn left and follow the path behind the farmhouse. Go gently uphill between trees to a stile, then turn left along a farm track. You can see from here the square chimneys of the house, its hung tiles and well-designed bargeboards over the gable, a typical Wealden farmhouse. Once an important milk herd of cattle was kept here. Now there are holiday cottages.

Follow the farm track to the right. You will soon see the Scots pines of Great Swifts on the skyline to the north. When you reach woods to your left you will see an old barn with interesting old beams. The track now turns left. You will see conifers growing on your right, part of a small plantation. Pass Moat Farm, with hung tiles on the upper storey. A small lion guards the corner of the garden. Go down to a stream with a metal fence along the bridge. This is the Crane Brook, which rises to the south-west. Walk on and up to the level ground where the farm track becomes metalled and make your way to the road. Turn right and walk beside the road for 150 yards.

Cross a stile on your right and go down a field path towards a hedge. Drop down into a small hollow between hawthorn, rowan and coppiced beech, then rise again and walk alongside a hedge towards some willows. Go down once more, to a footbridge, then rise to a field recently planted with willows. Follow the hedge line along the headland, round a wooded area surrounding a deep pond. Like many such ponds in the High Weald this pond was first formed to harness water power for ironworks, long vanished.

Turn left at the hedge line and walk up towards the grounds of Great Swifts. Not much of the hedge remains but you will see occasional small trees, such as hawthorn and elder. At the top, turn left through a gate set at an angle, into the path you first came along, and walk back to the road. As you return you see the windmill ahead to your left.

Turn right at the road and walk for 200 yards up to the inn.

Places of interest nearby

For details of *Cranbrook Mill*, telephone: 01580 712256.

Sissinghurst Gardens (National Trust) are open between April and October. Telephone: 01580 712850.

13 Hawkhurst
The Eight Bells

At The Moor you find the original Hawkhurst, ½ mile south of the modern centre. Its late-medieval church of St Laurence was built of ragstone blocks, five hundred years before the Victorian church by Sir Giles Gilbert Scott at Highgate. The peal of St Laurence's church rings out each week over the large green.

The Eight Bells at the south-eastern corner of the green takes its name from that peal. It has stood here since Elizabethan times and must have seen some of the skirmishes and plotting of smuggling days. Now, well refurbished after a serious fire, it has two bars, a restaurant and a large room with pool table, but retains many of its old beams.

To eat, you could choose from a good selection of bar food or one of the grills. Home-made pies are a speciality, the steak and kidney pudding being particularly popular. Fresh fish comes daily from Rye, so you will also find good seafood, cooked to order. The regular ales are brewed by Harveys and Bass. Guest ales change regularly, covering virtually all available. Lagers include Grolsch, and the coffee deserves special praise.

The inn is open from 11 am to 2.30 pm and 6 pm to 11 pm. Lunches are served daily from 12 noon to 2 pm. Dinners are served on Tuesday to Saturday from 7 pm to 9.30 pm.

Telephone: 01580 753233.

How to get there: From Flimwell on the A21, just south of the Bewl Bridge Reservoir, turn east for 3 miles along the A268. The Moor is ½ mile south on the A229. Or take the A229 east from the A21 ¼ mile north of Hurst Green.

Parking: There is a car park beside the inn.

Length of the walk: 3½ miles. OS maps: Landranger 188 Maidstone and The Weald of Kent, Pathfinder 1270 Robertsbridge and Broad Oak (inn GR 756295).

This walk takes you past St Laurence's church and along the lanes to the slopes above a small stream which drains these slopes. You then go gently downhill, with views ahead over traditional pasture to the Sussex border. You take a short stretch of the Sussex Border Path to Conghurst Farm and walk down a broad track, now with views towards Sandhurst. A small ghyll brings pheasants almost eating from your hand. You return over fields, turn into Conghurst Lane, then take Stream Lane back to The Moor.

The Walk

Turn left when you leave the inn. Go past the Old Bakehouse towards St Laurence's church. This, like most churches dating from the Middle Ages, reveals a mixture of tastes and styles as different generations added to it and repaired it. The oldest part is the chancel, from the 13th century. The nave was built in the next century, the tower later still. The best part is the east window, in Decorated style with wonderful sweeps in the tracery of its five lights. It is one of the finest in Kent.

Cross the A229 and go into Stream Lane. Turn right after 500 yards and continue to the track leading to East Heath. You will see the finch, sign of the Sussex Border Path, on a fence post.

If by any chance the track to East Heath is closed, for footbridge repairs, continue along Stream Lane, turn right into Conghurst Lane, then left at Conghurst Farm and continue ahead.

Whenever the track is open, go along it to East Heath, pass the oasts and continue on downhill along what was the old road from Sandhurst to The Moor, leaving the hedge on your left. Cross a bridge over the stream at the bottom, then go more steeply ahead, up the right side of the field. Go alongside Coach Hill Cottages and turn left onto the road. Walk for 100 yards. Leave Conghurst Lane to your left, then go straight ahead into the private road belonging to Conghurst Farm. The post is 'WC 248A' and you will see the Sussex Border Path sign on the upright. Carry on along this path past the converted triple oasts of Conghurst Oast and a small vineyard on the right.

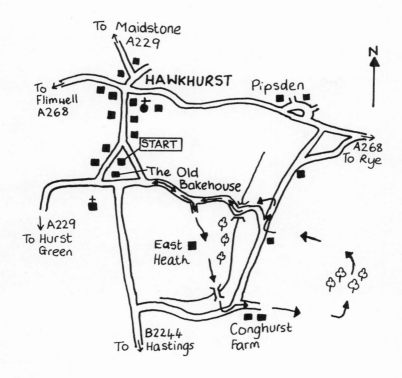

Pass Ragstone Barn, then go straight through Conghurst Farm and continue down the farm track. Lovely at any time of the year, the woodland areas look especially fine when clothed in their autumn colours. Ahead, to the east, lie Sandhurst Woods, to the south, Bodiam Woods. The Sussex border, marked by the Kent Ditch, runs east-west in the valley to your right.

After the first field walk ahead, following the yellow arrow. As you walk you will see standard oaks rising out of a hedge on your left. At the last oak, 350 yards beyond the farm, turn left and follow the headland, with hedge and bracken on your left, up the slope. Ahead, to your right, Downgate Woods stretch up the further slope. At the top left-hand corner of the field you will come to a wide gate. Go through this and ahead, down a sunken path. You will reach a pond, on your right, with a tangle of fallen trees stretching over it. The area is a paradise for pheasants. Go over the stream and up the next slope to a gate on your left. Turn through this and walk up the right-hand side of a broad field, with the hedge on your right, towards a gate. At the top you will have more good views in every direction.

St Laurence's church tower, near Hawkhurst.

Go through a gateway, past an attractive pond, along the level, then past a house and onto the road. Turn right into Conghurst Lane. At the corner of Conghurst Lane and Stream Lane you will find a well-situated seat with good views towards the first slope you descended, at East Heath. You can either turn left down Stream Lane or continue for 250 yards till you reach a public footpath sign at a stile, pointing down the field. This small extension is well worth while for yet another view.

Go slightly left down the field to a stile at the bottom, then turn right into Stream Lane. Go ahead, over the stream you passed before at Coach Hill Cottages, and up the next slope. When you reach Thorpes Farm, glance right at the twin octagonal cowls on the oasts. After 100 yards you pass the entrance to East Heath. Go ahead and follow the road back to the A229. Cross and continue to St Laurence's church. The inn is on your right.

Place of interest nearby

Bodiam Castle, owned by the National Trust, is $1\frac{1}{2}$ miles, as a crow flies, over the slope to the south in the Rother valley, $3\frac{1}{4}$ miles from The Moor by road. It is open all year, except 25th to 29th December. For times, telephone: 01580 830436.

14 Goudhurst
The Star and Eagle

The village of Goudhurst, 400 feet above sea level, sits on one of the highest ridges of the High Weald. From the churchyard of St Mary's you will enjoy extensive views over the slopes to the south.

The Star and Eagle, beside the churchyard, was once a monastery. In the 18th century, as an inn, it became the centre of a particularly vicious gang of smugglers. These were only defeated when a specially-raised band of militia engaged them in pitched battle in the street outside. Today, the inn is one of Whitbread's Wayside Inns and the bar and restaurants, with huge fireplaces and massive timbers, seem very remote from such times. The comfort and the welcome are superb for both adults and children.

The food is varied and good. All main courses are served with fresh vegetables or salad, local or home grown. Appetizers include butterfly breaded prawns with a peanut dip, and prawns in garlic butter. You could follow with breast of Barbarie duck or baked rainbow trout. Murphy's pie, with steak and mushrooms braised in stout and topped with pastry, gives warmth on a chilly day. If you wanted something lighter you could go for the generous portion of Stilton, Cheddar or Brie served with the ploughman's, have chilli con carne with rice or tagliatelle carbonara. Steaks come in all shapes and sizes from the griddle. The vegetarian may have provençale nut Wellington or vegetable Stroganoff. There are plenty of sticky puddings and mouth-watering ice creams. The children's menu offers a wide range of dishes. Real ales include Fremlins Bitter and Flowers Original. In rotation you will find Boddingtons or Harveys Bitter. Other strains of the hop are recalled in Glorious Goldings and Fuggles Chocolate Mild. There is also Strongbow cider as well as a good wine list.

The inn is open from 11 am to 11 pm on Monday to Saturday and from 11 am to 10.30 pm on Sunday.

Telephone: 01580 211512.

How to get there: Goudhurst is on the A262, 3 miles from the A21 and 4 miles west of the A229. The inn is next to the churchyard, on the west side, at the top of the High Street.

Parking: Turn south by the village pond, then first left to reach the car park behind the inn.

Length of the walk: 3 miles. OS maps: Landranger 188 Maidstone and The Weald of Kent, Pathfinder 1249 Wadhurst, Cranbrook and Bewl Bridge Reservoir (inn GR 723378).

This walk takes you along some slopes to the south of Goudhurst. You can see how the use of the land has changed here, where hop gardens once took over from ironworks. Now land is being set aside and buildings converted. You see a horse track and a water jump, then ascend to return along the delightful main street of Goudhurst.

The Walk

Leave the inn by the back door. Turn left out of the parking area and, 20 paces ahead, turn right and walk downhill past the cemetery. You can see oast houses in the valley ahead. Lines of poplars help to create the patchwork of fields so characteristic of the High Weald. At the bottom of the field go over the stile and down some steps onto the road.

Turn left to a junction a few paces ahead, then double back along the lower road. Walk past Maypole Cottage on your left, with hung tiles and half-timbered porch. At the bend, where you meet the B2079, turn left along the public footpath and walk between a converted barn on the left, Whites Cottage and Whites Farmhouse on your right.

The path continues downhill between pasture and paddocks. At a row of four recently converted houses go ahead down a cart track for 150 yards. When the main track swings to the right as footpath 'WC 43', turn left and follow 'WC 44' ahead, down the slope into a

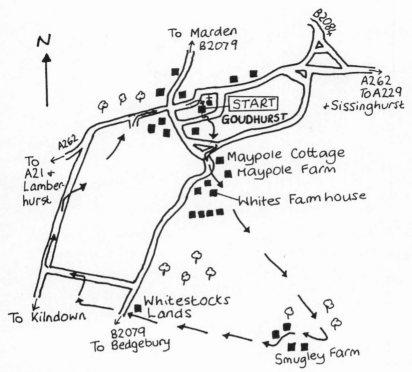

field. Walk ahead along the left-hand side of the field. Cross a farm track and continue, with a shaw on your left. Leave the headland when it swings to the left and go downhill to the ghyll. Follow a yellow marker round a tree, then cross a solid bridge over the stream.

Now walk diagonally right, up the hill. You should aim for a space in the hedge line at the top, some 50 yards to the left of the apex of the field. When you reach this point and look back you will see how St Mary's church dominates the skyline. Go through the gap in the hedge and follow the arrow ahead. Cross a farm track which leads to the right, to Smugley Farm, then cross a very narrow bridge and go straight ahead, keeping a shaw on your left-hand side, that is, the eastern side of the field.

The right of way follows the line of this shaw to a track 500 yards ahead at the top. The field may be slightly overgrown but the going is steady. When you reach the track turn round and re-cross the field, this time aiming for the north-western side of the woods beside Smugley Farm. To do this, walk towards the point of woodland which comes out some 300 yards ahead on your left.

Join a farm track which comes in from the right. This is the track you

The village pond at Goudhurst.

passed by the very narrow bridge. Now follow it ahead, making for the outhouses of Smugley Farm. Continue towards a converted, brown, weatherboarded barn, Smugley Barn. Turn left, follow the track along, down and round to the right of recently-converted oasts, then turn sharp right. Pass Smugley Farmhouse, a Wealden house with hung tiles and brick under storey, on your right.

Walk for 600 yards along a metalled track to the road. On the way you will see, between the trees, hop gardens rising up the left-hand slope. On your right you pass a small farm at Whitestocks Lands. Cross the road and go down some steps to a ghyll. Go over a stile into a field, then cross the field, keeping the hedge on your left-hand side. You will see a fine, half-timbered Wealden house, Pattenden Farm, on your left. Built in the late Middle Ages, it escaped the hung tiles which cover the upper storey of so many older houses.

At the far side of the field, leave by a wide, ungated exit and turn immediately right through a large metal gate. Turn left, continue the line you have been taking and cross this field to a similar gate. As you cross you will see below a track designed for cross-country riding.

Square oasts, such as you see at Risebridge Farm ahead, were used for a time in the 18th century until it was felt that the round form led to better drying conditions for the hops.

Go through the gate and, again, turn immediately right, through another gate. Follow the fence and hedge up the right-hand side of the field, round the side of a copse, to a stile. Cross this and turn left onto the road. At the crossroads turn right to Goudhurst. Pass two houses on your left. After Thatchers Hall, to your right, turn right and follow the public footpath between hedges to a stile. You now go across fields to the edge of Goudhurst, crossing another stile on the way.

To the right you have splendid views south over the valley. To the left, over the brow of the hill, you can just make out the wooded slopes beside Horsmonden.

At the far side of the field, cross a final stile into a narrow path between houses. Emerge onto Lurkins Rise. Turn left to the A262. From here you can see St Margaret's church at Horsmonden, below the trees. Turn right, walk the last ¼ mile back to Goudhurst along the main road and enjoy the way the village spreads out round its church-topped summit.

Allow time to visit the church, if you can. Essentially medieval, St Mary's contains a variety of styles, introduced as the fortunes of Goudhurst increased. In the Bedgebury Chapel you will see a marble monument to four generations of Culpepers who lived at Bedgebury and made their fortune as ironmasters.

Places of interest nearby

Also worth visiting in the area is *Bedgebury National Pinetum*, which lies 3 miles south of Goudhurst, off the B2079. Telephone: 01580 211044.

Finchcocks, 2 miles to the south-west, beside the A262, houses a fascinating museum of musical instruments. Telephone: 01580 211702.

15 West Farleigh
The Tickled Trout

West Farleigh straddles the slopes above the Medway in the middle of fruit-growing country, little more than 3 miles from Maidstone.

The Tickled Trout still has its original timber frame. Now much restored, and run by Whitbread's, it offers a well-run restaurant and a good area for eating near the bar. A nautical air, with fishing nets and fancy knots, recalls the inn's name and the fisherman painted on the outside wall. Beside is a pleasant garden, which runs along beside the road. Children are welcome in the restaurant. You will find a regular set menu, which includes a good ploughman's lunch and sandwiches, as well as the more usual scampi or chicken dishes. There is also a full à la carte menu. Among the 'specials' are steaks and, in particular, fish dishes such as salmon cutlet or grilled trout. Fremlins, Flowers and Wadworth 6X are on hand-pump, or you might well try something from the good wine list.

The Tickled Trout is open seven days a week, 11 am to 3 pm and 6 pm to 11 pm on Monday to Saturday. On Sunday it is open from 12 noon to 3 pm and from 7 pm to 10.30 pm.

Telephone: 01622 812589.

How to get there: The Tickled Trout is reached from the A26 Tonbridge to Maidstone road. Turn south on the B2163 at Teston. Fork right after $1/2$ mile. The inn is on your right, 200 yards further on.

Parking: The car park is on the right-hand side of the inn, at the back.

Length of the walk: $3^1/2$ miles. OS maps: Landranger 188 Maidstone and The Weald of Kent, Pathfinder 1209 Maidstone (inn GR 713527).

This walk takes you down the slopes above the Medway, through grazing and pasture, to the old bridge at Teston. You then turn west to walk for $1^1/2$ miles to Wateringbury, along the Medway towpath. You cross at Wateringbury and return on the opposite bank, through a stretch of ancient woodland. The path takes you gently uphill, then through a farm and orchards before regaining the road at West Farleigh. This is a scenic and attractive walk, where you will see willows overhanging the water and interesting bird life. The towpath is well frequented by fishermen and also by those who like to watch small boats.

The Walk
Turn right when you leave the inn and walk past the garden. Turn right again through a metal kissing gate and follow the path down past the back of the pub. Now veer to the right and make for the far right-hand

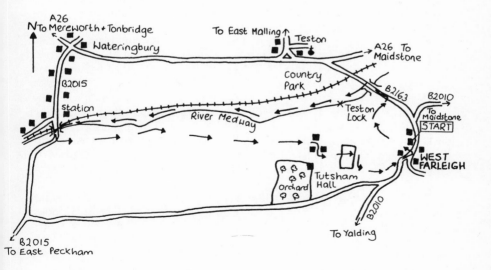

The Medway, Teston.

corner of the field. As you approach the corner you go under a row
of pollarded limes. Climb over a stile. Turn right and head for the next
stile, but do not cross it. Instead, turn left and go down the tree line to a
gate. Cross the stile and go ahead along a metalled track. Turn right, then
cross the B2163 and follow the footpath over the bridge. Make use of the
niches originally intended for packhorses, if the traffic requires it.

Immediately after the bridge, you will see a stile on your left with
'Medway River Project' written on it. Climb over the stile and make
your way down to the river. This area is part of Teston Country Park.
Turn right and go towards Teston Lock, the third of ten locks on the
Medway between Allington and Tonbridge. It was built in 1740 by the
Medway Navigation Company to help the transport of iron and timber
down the Medway to the Thames.

Go through the first of a series of kissing gates. When you are level
with the trees on the opposite bank, the path veers to your right, away
from the river. Go through another kissing gate at the boundary of
Teston Park and continue ahead.

Go through two more gates, moving away from the river for a while
and towards the railway, then rejoin the river and continue along
a broader track past a number of moored boats. Ahead you see
the railway buildings and the bridge at Wateringbury. Pass alongside the
cream-painted Bow Bridge Marina. Go through the gate and up the

path to the Wateringbury signal box. Turn left over the bridge. You will see the Medway Wharf Marina diagonally opposite on your right. Just after its entrance you will find a gate, approached by a cattle grid, to your left. Go over the stile beside it and head across the field, along a clearly-trodden track, with a fence on your left.

Cross a series of stiles until you come to a small bridge with another stile at the end. Continue ahead to Waregraves Wood, a valuable conservation area containing coppiced ash and interesting wildlife. A well-found path leads you on for 300 yards to a stile at the far end of the woods.

Go over the stile and walk up a grassy slope to the level. You will pass the concrete footing of an old building. Follow the grassy path up to the right. Make for the gate in the top left-hand corner, then turn to a stile in the fence which runs down towards the Medway. You will see orchards ahead to the right. Now walk towards, then past, a barn. Cross the cattle grid and go up the farm track past farm buildings. Ignore the path arrowed left, downhill, and go ahead, alongside the fence, towards more farm buildings. Turn right up the driveway towards Tutsham Hall, then left, past a barn. Walk ahead, leaving apple orchards on your left.

Go through a gate into an orchard and follow the path which winds ahead to another gate 150 yards ahead. Go through, then turn right and follow a farm track to a third gate. Enter some more orchards, where you will see pear trees to the left, apples to the right. At the top turn left into a broad track and walk between farm buildings. You will see a weatherboarded barn on your left. Go down the metalled driveway, leaving some stables to your right.

Turn left onto Smith's Hill and walk past the junction on your right. The Tickled Trout is 200 yards ahead on your left.

16 Little Mill
The Man of Kent

The tiny hamlet, one mile from East Peckham and beside the river Bourne, became known as Little Mill to distinguish it from the large mill at Branbridges, further down the Medway. You can see what is left of the mill if you stand on the bridge and look upstream.

The Man of Kent, a Grade II listed building, was established here in 1588. Once a private house with a cottage alongside, it still has some of the old beams, so low that anyone over 6 ft tall should duck before entering. The pub is small and unpretentious and gives a warm welcome to all. Families may eat in the dining area and in the lounge away from the bar. The terrace beside the river is a popular place, especially in summer. The name 'Man of Kent' is a reminder of the old distinction between those who lived to the east of the Medway and the Kentish Men who lived to the west.

The menu includes a range of starters and main meals, such as chicken Kiev, a good cannelloni and plaice and chips. For real ales you will find Bass, Harveys Sussex Best, Fremlins and Charrington IPA. Winterwarmer is on offer through the colder months. Lagers include Grolsch, Pilsner, Carling Black Label and Budweiser. Red Rock Dry cider is on draught, and Toby Keg Bitter.

The Man of Kent is open on weekdays from 11 am to 2.30 pm and from 6 pm to 11 pm, on Saturdays from 11 am to 3 pm and from 6 pm to 11 pm, and on Sundays from 12 noon to 3 pm and 7 pm to 10.30 pm. Food is served throughout the week, except on Monday evening. Telephone: 01622 871345.

How to get there: Little Mill lies along minor roads between the A26, north of Tonbridge, and the A228 (formerly the B2015). Turn west off the A228 (2¼ miles north of Paddock Wood) into East Peckham. About ⅓ mile ahead turn left to Snoll Hatch. Go sharp right at Snoll Hatch, then first left, then ahead for ½ mile. The Man of Kent is on the right, just after the bridge.

Parking: You can park beside the pub and at the back.

Length of the walk: 1⅞ miles or 2⅞ miles if you extend the walk to Sluice Weir Lock. OS maps: Landranger 188 Maidstone and The Weald of Kent, Pathfinder 1229 Paddock Wood and Staplehurst (inn GR 657482).

The walk takes you across the fields beside the Medway, over one of the large Medway footbridges, along the Medway towpath and back to Little Mill, alongside the diminutive but important river Bourne. Now the land is largely arable, but once the entire area bore hop gardens and fruit orchards.
There is also a chance to see Sluice Weir Lock, once an important part of the Medway Navigation. You may encounter mud after wet weather and boots are recommended then, but this is an attractive walk at any time of the year.

The Walk

Turn right out of the pub, along what used to be the old highway from Maidstone to Tonbridge. Walk along the road to the last house on the left, an attractive cottage with a steep roof and hung tiles. Turn left and take the broad path between hedges. A clear sign points to the river Medway, ½ mile away. About 100 yards past the house, South Stilstead, you will see a double gate. Go through the space on the right, follow the arrow marked 'Medway River Project' and continue along the track, with wide fields to the right and left.

To the north you can see the eastern and western sections of the Greensand Ridge. The Medway cuts through the gap on its way to the Thames. These floodplains owe their fertility to the silt brought down after rain from the High Weald. The entire area used to suffer serious flooding in wet weather as water drained off the clay slopes of

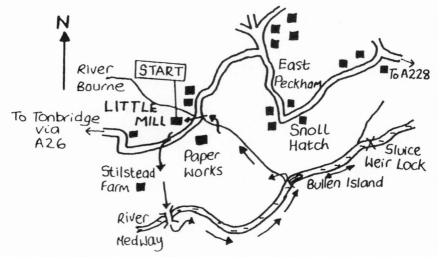

the High Weald and the Medway overflowed. This problem only ceased in 1979/80 with the building of the Medway flood barrier at Haysden, 1¾ miles west of Tonbridge.

Soon you will pass a narrow shaw on your left, which protects the Medway side of the field from easterly winds. Continue past a gate on your right to a concrete bridge. Its unsightly metal railings are more than offset by the shapely willow overhanging the bank on your right. Cross the bridge to the sturdy wooden fingerpost at the far side. This shows several routes, all offering good walks. Take the route signed left to 'Branbridges', 1½ miles away. Avoid the broad track which leads into woodland and go further left along the footpath beside the river. You will see a yellow marker confirming this route as you get close to the river.

You now follow the Medway River Path for ¾ mile. This is a narrow path, which often drops straight down to the river on the left-hand side. Boots or shoes with a firm grip are essential in wet weather.

You pass beside woodland on your right for ¼ mile. At the end of this stretch you cross a stile. As you emerge from the woodland you will see a post on your right with arrows pointing in every direction. Simply continue along the river bank, passing a broad field to your right. At the end you reach a shaw with old tree trunks well covered by moss. Go past a large chestnut post at the point where the path touches the edge of the field. Carry along the edge of the field, making for the bridge ahead, then follow the field along the edge of the river.

At a large metal post, surmounted with a white band, turn left to cross a stile leading onto a small wooden bridge. This bridge takes you over a small channel, formed as the Medway cut Bullen Island off from the main field. Now continue to a very sturdy footbridge over the Medway itself.

If you want to take a longer walk and visit the lock gates at Sluice Weir Lock, go straight ahead here. Continue along a broad grassy track to another wooden bridge, which has been very well repaired. Take a short turn to the right to a marker post and follow the arrow along the edge of the next field. Halfway along, step left and down to the river bank. This is a wonderful area for flowers and birds in spring. About ½ mile from Bullen Island you reach Sluice Weir Lock. This was built in the mid-18th century by the Medway Navigation Company and became the fifth lock up the Medway. At this time the Medway offered an ideal way of bringing timber and iron downstream from the High Weald. East Peckham and Branbridges formed a busy inland port. A series of locks at the sluice and the sight of oast houses in the distance make this an intriguing part of mid-Kent. Retrace your steps to the bridge over the Medway, to return to the inn.

To continue the circular route, cross the bridge and walk beside the narrow tributary, the Bourne, which you first met at Little Mill. The path is now a little further from the water than before. In spite of its small size, this little river, which rises near Ightham on the Greensand Ridge, has in its day provided enough water power for several mills along its way.

The Sluice Weir Lock near Little Mill.

At the next stile, turn left and cross the Bourne. Good railings offset the narrowness of the bridge here and prevent vertigo. Turn right and follow the footpath alongside the Bourne until you reach another bridge, crossing back to the right-hand side once more. This brings you to the last house at the end of a lane. The field to the right used to be called Cage Field as it once contained the local pound.

You should turn left here, walk along the lane past the row of houses and return to the bridge at Little Mill. The bridge was built in 1575 when a mill owner dug too deep a watercourse and made it impossible for travellers to ford the small stream.

Place of interest nearby

You can see something of the area's agricultural heritage at the *Whitbread Hop Farm* at Beltring, situated beside the A228, to the south.

17 Lamberhurst
The Chequers

Lamberhurst is alongside the river Teise, in the heart of the High Weald. This friendly pub, full of character and situated beside the main road, was originally a 14th-century coaching house and provided a vital stop on the three-day journey from London to Hastings. Its oak beams and inglenook fireplace combine to make it a most attractive and welcoming place from which to visit the neighbouring area of the High Weald. There are tables away from the immediate bar area, but near the fireplace, as well as in the dining room and families are welcome. You will find a small garden with tables beside the river, as well as a children's play area (no dogs allowed), with swings and climbing frame, at the back, adjoining open fields. The Chequers is now owned by Shepherd Neame.

The food is home-made and excellent, with a good regular menu and a wide range of special dishes, which change daily. Particularly recommended are the home-made soups, the cheese and onion quiche and the steak and kidney pie. All come with fresh vegetables and sauté or creamed potatoes. Puddings, especially the cherry and apricot flan and the treacle tart, are dangerously tempting. Here you can drink Shepherd Neame Master Brew and Spitfire. Lagers include Hürlimann's and Steinbok, and Dry Blackthorn and Scrumpy Jack ciders are available.

The Chequers is open from 11 am to 3 pm and from 5.45 pm until 'late'. On Sundays it opens between 11.30 am and 3 pm, then again from 7 pm to 10.30 pm.
Telephone: 01892 890260.

How to get there: Lamberhurst is on the A21, 1 mile south of the junction with the A262. The Chequers is on the east side of the road, immediately south of the river Teise.

Parking: There is a parking area immediately behind the pub, reached from the south side. Next to that is also a public car park.

Length of the walk: 1½ miles. OS maps: Landranger 188 Maidstone and The Weald of Kent, Pathfinder 1249 Wadhurst, Cranbrook and Bewl Bridge Reservoir (inn GR 677363).

This walk takes you by well-trodden footpaths along the slopes of rolling countryside, amidst the typically Wealden scenery that flanks the river Teise. The walk is short and gives time to visit the 14th-century church of St Mary and then go on by car to visit Scotney Castle or the nearby Lamberhurst Vineyards. You may extend the walk by turning off to follow clearly signed paths in the grounds of Scotney Castle.

The Walk

Follow the signed footpath in the stone block to the left of the outhouses behind the car park. Make your way through the garden area and enter the playing field. You now move away from the river and cross the first playing field, heading diagonally to the right. Make for two oak trees and pass to their right through a gap in the old hedge line. You will see another children's play area on the right-hand side at the beginning of the second playing field.

Make your way to the far right-hand corner of this field and climb over the stile. Walk alongside a hedge for a few paces, then cross the golf course to another stile. Look carefully to the right to check that no one is playing towards you. Go over the next stile, which you will find set into the hedge line just before it ends. After a further 100 yards cross another fairway.

Cross a stile in the hedge into a field. The root of a large tree trunk blocks the official right of way, so use the well-trodden path leading straight ahead, take a few steps along a concrete farm road, then turn right and walk along the headland of a wedge-shaped field, leaving the hedge on your left-hand side and passing under a spreading oak tree. Turn left at a wide field entrance and walk up the headland, leaving the woods to your right.

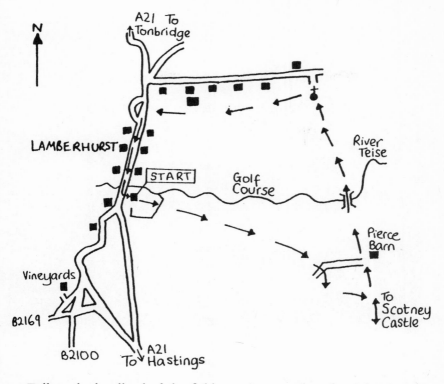

Follow the headland of the field, curving round to the right. As you turn sharply right around the bend look across the valley to St Mary's church, which nestles on the further hillside. The slopes, hop gardens and woodland combine to make it one of the classic views of the High Weald.

Continue your way round and up to the top. Here you will see a sign pointing you to the right, to National Trust land and towards Scotney Castle. You may well want to walk in the woods surrounding the National Trust property. Alternatively, you may prefer to go later by car, in which case you will be able to see the castle, not visible from the public rights of way.

To continue the walk, turn left at the top of the slope, and walk down the hedge line towards the concrete farm road. At the bottom of the field you will reach a stile with no risers. Cross this and the concrete track, then head downhill across the next field along a well-trodden path. At the bottom you will find a small bridge over the Teise.

In dry weather this little river hardly looks the important tributary of the Medway that it certainly is. It can be a different matter in wet

A Kent hop garden.

weather, when it drains the water flowing off the clay slopes of the region. The Teise used to power many ironworks along its way and was a strong factor behind the flooding which often occurred lower down on the Medway.

Cross the bridge and head up the next field towards the church. At the top you come to the edge of St Mary's churchyard. Pass between two posts then turn immediately left to skirt the churchyard.

The church and churchyard are well worth visiting. You will see an old 'mass dial' on the buttress of the south wall, an unusual perpendicular doorway and, inside, numerous memorials to the Thomas family. Outside, you will see several intriguing tombs. Note the Prickett tombs on the left of the path beside the church door, and the attendant angel. The yew tree is said to be 1,500 years old.

To continue the walk, return to the path below the churchyard and turn onto the path which leads across the top of the golf course. Follow this as it leads in a straight line towards the main road. Continue ahead until you emerge onto the A21 beside a small triangle of grass. Turn left and walk down the main road, cross the Teise and return to the Chequers.

Places of interest nearby

Scotney Castle is reached from the A21, just south of Lamberhurst, on the way to Hastings. Telephone: 01892 890651.

The *Lamberhurst Vineyards* are to be found on the south side of the B2169, which runs west on the south side of the village. Founded in 1972, the vineyards cover 60 acres of the hillside and produce a wide range of wines. You can walk in the vineyards throughout the year and between May and October you may join guided tours of the winery and cellars. Telephone: 01892 890286.

Speldhurst
The George and Dragon

Situated in the centre of Speldhurst village, 2 miles west of Southborough, the George and Dragon was first built in 1212. Soldiers returning from the battle of Agincourt in 1415 revelled there after their victory over the French. In the 18th century smugglers may have used a tunnel between the pub and the church to make their escape whenever news came that the militia were on their way. Today you can see some of the old beams inside – and enjoy the food, which ranks among the best.

You may eat in the bar area or in the buttery, where children are very welcome. Dressed Cornish crab and chargrilled Cajun chicken breast are regulars on the menu. The steak, kidney and Guinness pie is particularly attractive on a cold winter's day. You will find a good selection of drinks. Worthington Best Bitter, Bass, Dry Blackthorn cider, Carling Black Label, Harveys Sussex Best, Harveys Sussex Pale Ale, Fuller's London Pride and Young's Special are all on offer, as well as Grolsch Premium lager and Caffrey's Irish Ale.

The George and Dragon is open all day on Monday to Saturday from 10.30 am to 11 pm. Food is served from 12 noon to 2.30 pm and from 7 pm to 10 pm. On Sunday it is open from 12 noon to 3 pm and 7 pm to 10.30 pm, with food from 12 noon to 3 pm.

Telephone: 01892 863125.

How to get there: Take the Speldhurst road from the A26 (Tonbridge to Tunbridge Wells road) at Southborough. The George and Dragon is 1¾ miles along this road, on the left. Alternatively, approach from the A264 (Tunbridge Wells to East Grinstead road), turning north at Langton Green. Turn right at the church and the inn is almost immediately on your right.

Parking: Parking is available in the area to the left of the inn.

Length of the walk: 2 miles. OS maps: Landranger 188 Maidstone and The Weald of Kent, Pathfinder 1228 Tonbridge and Edenbridge (inn GR 554415).

This walk takes you through the old village of Speldhurst, past some fine listed buildings and on into open countryside typical of the High Weald. You can see how the wooded, rolling hills are frequently intersected by narrow, often steep-sided, ghylls. The slopes of Shadwell Wood itself are a joy in bluebell season and rich in wildlife at any time of the year. You will walk along part of an old coach road. You can also visit the impressive church of St Mary the Virgin.

Speldhurst village.

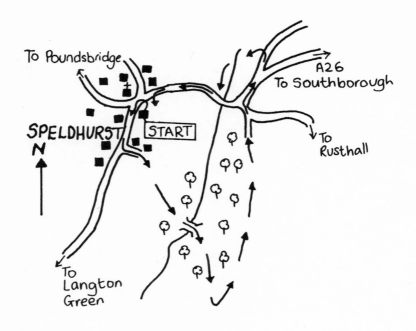

The Walk

On leaving the pub cross the road, turn left and walk beside the churchyard wall to the church gate. The church of St Mary the Virgin, rebuilt in the 19th century, contains some of the best Burne-Jones and William Morris windows in the country. Over the doorway you will see the coat of arms of the French duke who, while a hostage in England, gave money for the rebuilding of the medieval church. In the churchyard both the tombstones and the lichens growing there are of considerable interest.

At the church gate turn down the Tunbridge Wells and Langton road. Go to the last house on your left, Shadwell, with hung tiles and a half-timbered porch. Turn left between this house and the open fields. You will see a signpost indicating the High Weald Link walk to Rusthall. Continue along the metalled track until the last house lies directly ahead of you.

Turn right into a broad, hedge-lined lane. This bends to the left after 20 yards. Climb over the stile into a narrow pathway between the two fields. Follow the path down the slope to another stile, which leads you into Shadwell Wood. Go down a short flight of shallow steps cut into the hillside, then continue downhill along a broad woodland path. Soon you reach a damp flush near to a spring. The flush is well covered with pieces of timber and has a small 'bridge' to protect you. You then cross the stream by a narrow bridge, just wide enough for one person, with iron rails. After heavy rain the stream will carry a strong force of water.

Bear right and make your way up the opposite slope, at an angle, until you come to a junction of four tracks, with the High Weald Walk sign pointing ahead. Leave others to take that route. Instead, take a sharp turn to the left so that you almost double back on yourself. You will now find yourself on a broad, sandy path, which runs along the upper slopes of the hillside. This was once an old coach road.

The area is still recovering from the damage caused by the hurricane of October 1987. You will notice, first of all, low scrub with standard trees in the hedgerow. Then, as the ground immediately below you clears, you can see coppicing on the other slope. Later, you go through thicker woodland where you will find tall beeches.

Where you see a division of tracks, continue on the main path, which bends slightly to the right. Make your way downhill over a path where sandy soil fills the spaces between protruding sandstone. In wet weather this track helps to drain the banks above, so be prepared to take this stretch carefully. Note the roots of beeches above you. About $1/2$ mile from the junction of the four tracks you will reach the road.

Turn left and go down the hill to a triangle at a junction of three roads. From here you would find the inn $1/2$ mile ahead, but to continue the main walk turn right into the Southborough-Speldhurst road, then left from this at another small triangle of grass and walk up the narrower of the two roads, signed to 'Stockland Green' and 'Southborough Common'. Just after the 'road narrows' sign you will see a tree stump in the right-hand bank, signing the Wealdway and the High Weald Walk. Follow the sign to the left, cross the forecourt of Forge House and enter a narrow lane which leads ahead, downhill. Continue on this lane over the stiles until you reach the courtyard of an animal food suppliers.

The weatherboarded watermill on your left is a rare survivor from the days when the Weald was a major corn producer. The wheel, now covered with moss, was driven as the water pushed buckets hanging from the blades.

Walk straight ahead up the slope, then follow the private road to the left. Continue for 200 yards until you reach the road from Southborough to Speldhurst. Cross the road to the pavement, turn right and make your way uphill. Pass Barden Road on your right, and continue for the last 100 yards back to the George and Dragon. On your way you will pass the Manor House. It was here that Robert Baden-Powell wrote *Scouting for Boys*.

⑲ Penshurst
The Leicester Arms

Penshurst lies on the edge of the High Weald, in the Upper Medway valley. Nearby is Penshurst Place, once home of Sir William Sidney, grandfather of the Elizabethan poet and statesman, Sir Philip Sidney. The Leicester Arms was named after the other grandson of Sir William, Viscount Lisle, appointed Earl of Leicester in 1618.

The inn's creeper-clad walls have a central place in the village. Inside, there are comfortable tables near the bar and more beyond. At the back, overlooking fields beside the Medway, is a large dining room. Children are very welcome. The quality and range of food is good. A typical day might offer home-made steak and kidney pudding, Barnsley chops, roast of the day or home-made lasagne. The special menu could include pork, chicken Kiev or lamb steak with garlic and rosemary. Home-made apple and blackcurrant crumble could follow, or chocolate sponge pudding. The two chief real ales are Boddingtons and Fremlins Bitter. You will also find Fuggles Chocolate, Wadworth 6X and Murphy's Irish Stout, in rotation with others. The cider is Scrumpy Jack, the lager is Heineken. There is a good wine list, too.

The inn is open from 11 am to 11 pm on Monday to Saturday, and from 12 noon to 3 pm and 7 pm to 10.30 pm on Sunday. Meals are

served seven days a week from 12 noon to 2 pm and from 7 pm to 9.30 pm.
Telephone: 01892 870551.

How to get there: From the A26 (between Tonbridge and Tunbridge Wells) take the B2176 westwards through Bidborough. Penshurst is reached after 3¹/₂ miles.

Parking: Parking is available behind the inn.

Length of the walk: 3 miles. OS maps: Landranger 188 Maidstone and The Weald of Kent, Pathfinder 1228 Tonbridge and Edenbridge (inn GR 527438).

This walk takes you through the village, through Leicester Square and past the church. You will see Penshurst Place from the outside, then take the old coach road which connected Penshurst with Hever, along the slopes above the river Eden. You return along other slopes, on good paths all the way.

The Walk
Turn right when you step out of the pub and walk on until you come to a path which rises above the road. Go up this and turn left into the small, three-sided square known as Leicester Square. Walk under the arch formed by the buildings overhanging, then turn left up the church path.

The sandstone church of St John the Baptist is most distinctive and unusual, with a tower surmounted by pinnacles rising from its four corners. You can see the Leicester arms once more, carved over the entrance to the church.

Go past the church and on up a small lane until you come to a stile. Cross this into a field and take the footpath, signed for the Eden Valley Walk, which runs diagonally left across the field towards the road.

You can see the outside of Penshurst Place as you walk. Cross a stile onto the road, watching carefully for the traffic. Turn left towards Penshurst until you come to a green junction box. Turn right towards Salmans Farm and follow this road to a bridge over the river Eden. You will pass a small pill box beside the road. You will also notice drainage ditches on either side of this road.

The river Eden rises near Lingfield in Surrey and joins the Medway just south of Penshurst. The measuring rod, marked for up to 32 metres, beside the Eden near the bridge gives an indication of the flooding that may sometimes happen.

Just after the bridge, the road to Salmans Farm bends to the left. Here you will see a farm track leading up the right-hand slope. Beside the track is a sign for the Eden Valley Walk confirming the route along this path. Follow this track as it curves its way along the slope above the river Eden. This was once the direct route from Penshurst Place to Hever Castle. As you walk you have good views north and east. Converted oast houses along the slopes show that the area was once covered with hop gardens. Continue between hedges of hawthorn, elder and oaks.

Just under 1 mile from the turning you will reach Wat Stock. Go through the farmyard until you pass the main house, on the left, and turn left into a broad track. This passes some cottages on the left, then bends to the right past a pond. About ½ mile further on the road bends to the right, becoming metalled as you pass Abbotsmerry Barn. You now drop downhill slightly more steeply, passing Salmans Farm on your left. You will see four converted oasts ahead, two with vanes distinctive for their figures, one of a blacksmith, the other of a driver with horse and cart. On your right, at Watermill Oast, you pass a duck pond and small heronry. The whole makes an attractive complex.

At the bottom of the slope turn left, then immediately right, along a narrow path which runs between a solid wooden fence and a post-and-rail fence. This forms a diversion from the former right of way marked on the Pathfinder map, revised in 1981. You will see, as you emerge, a house to your right, with tiles, chimneys and gables. At the end go

Leicester Square, Penshurst.

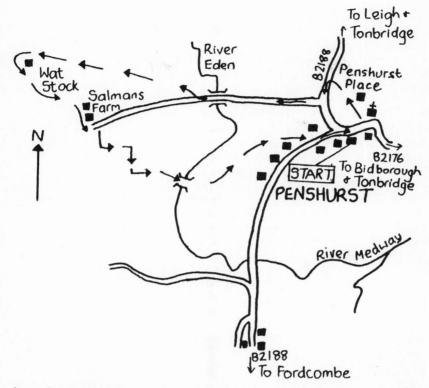

through a gateway, turn left, then climb over a stile, situated to the left of a metal gate, into a field.

Walk across the field, keeping to the headland, with the hedge on your left-hand side. Cross into the next field and continue, straight ahead, to follow the right of way to the strip of woodland at the far side. Turn right, keeping the trees and hedge to your left and continue to a stile 150 yards ahead, at a point where the hedge line starts to bend to the right. Turn left into a narrow path between a fence of chestnut paling and a hedge. You will see a new plantation of mixed woodland trees on your right. At the end a narrow footbridge takes you over the Eden into a small field. Cross this field on a diagonal line to the right and climb over another stile into a field which takes you gently upwards to some higher ground.

To the left and north you will see a small hop garden. Behind you, to the south-west, the thickly wooded hill rises to over 300 feet. On the slope to your right, to the south-east, you can see a group of buildings with ornate gables. These are at Home Farm and were designed in the 19th century by George Devey, who worked to revive rustic architecture.

As the slope levels off you see farm buildings ahead. Cross a stile and follow the path as it winds right, towards a barn. Leave a wooden granary and stabling to your left and walk straight ahead, ignoring a broad track to your right. Go past West Farm Cottage and West Farm. To your left the slope drops sharply before levelling out to the flat stretch where you walked earlier.

Ahead you see the battlements, turrets and pinnacles of Penshurst's church. Continue for $1/2$ mile until you reach the B2188. Turn left and walk the last 300 yards to the Leicester Arms.

Place of interest nearby

Penshurst Place is open seven days a week from the end of March to the beginning of October and every Saturday and Sunday in March and October. The gardens and venture playground are open from 11 am to 6 pm and the house is open between 12 noon and 5.30 pm (last entry 5 pm). Telephone: 01892 870307.

⓴ Hever
The King Henry VIII

The King Henry VIII stands on the one corner of Hever village, opposite the lovely, Grade I listed, St Peter's church. Nearby stands Hever Castle, where Henry VIII's courtship of Anne Boleyn was to change the course of English history.

Inside the inn, old beams and, on cold days, a wood fire burning in a large fireplace set the atmosphere. Motifs on curtains and carpets recall the monarch and you will see, framed on the walls, some of the letters that went between him and Anne Boleyn. Children are welcome in the restaurant area and there is a pleasant garden with an attractive pond.

The range of meals is appealing. You could choose from a variety of seafoods, or have savoury spare ribs or the broccoli and potato bake. You could also have real ale chutney with the quiche. Children's portions are available. Old Henry Castle Bitter (brewed by Ruddles for the pub) heads the real ale list. You will also find Adnams Southwold Bitter, draught Beamish and Harveys Sussex Best Bitter. Foster's and Kronenbourg 94 are available and there is a good range of wines.

The inn is open on weekdays from 11 am to 3 pm and from 6 pm to 11 pm, and on Sundays from 12 noon to 3 pm and 6 pm to 10.30 pm.

Telephone: 01732 862163.

How to get there: Hever is 10 miles west of Tonbridge and 3 miles east of Edenbridge. Take the road signed to 'Hever', which runs west beside the railway bridge at Bough Beech, at the junction of the B269 and the B2027. The King Henry VIII is situated 2½ miles to the south.

Parking: Parking is available, for patrons of the inn, on the other side of the road, to the south. The other park in the village is reserved for coaches visiting the castle and should not be used.

Length of the walk: 2½ miles. OS maps: Landranger 188 Maidstone and The Weald of Kent, Pathfinder 1228 Tonbridge and Edenbridge (inn GR 475448).

This walk takes you out past the historic church of St Peter, along a short stretch of the Eden Valley Walk. It then circles back to take you onto slightly higher slopes above the river Eden. Here you have views north to the Greensand Ridge and south over the rolling, wooded slopes that surround the area.

The Walk

Take the path, signed for the Eden Valley Walk, through the churchyard. St Peter's stands on the site of an older, Norman church. The north aisle and part of the nave of today's church were first built in 1292. It contains some exceptional monumental brasses. One, to Sir Thomas Bullen, father of Anne Boleyn and grandfather of Queen Elizabeth I, lies on his tomb in a chapel dedicated to the family. Another, even older, is on the floor of the chancel, with angels at the head, in memory of Margaret Cheyne who died in 1419.

Go to the end of the churchyard, then follow the earthen path down into a shallow dip. Walk along a path under a hedge, past houses, and continue alongside an avenue. Between the trees you will get glimpses of the lake at Hever Castle. To the north you will see the Greensand Ridge. Follow the path round the corner, between fences of chestnut paling. You now find woodland on your right, containing sycamore and rowan. Cross a narrow wooden bridge over a small road and follow a grass path. Now you will see young birch trees growing on your right. The path soon joins a road, then runs beside it for 200 yards. Follow it to the left and continue for 300 yards to a gateway.

Carry on to the swinging gate, which bears the Eden Valley Walk sign. Turn back 20 paces, past a house with hung tiles, to join a grassy path which runs between fences towards woodland. Cross a stile into the first of three fields, linked by stiles, which run for ½ mile along a ridge.

From the ridge you will find splendid, rolling views, first to the slopes

of the Eden valley to the east and south-east, then to Ide Hill on the Greensand Ridge. You also get glimpses of the North Downs.

In the third field the right of way follows the hedge line, rising slightly, at the edge of woodland at the top of the field, then taking a sharp turn to the left. At this point you get good views down the slope on your right to the grounds of Hever Castle. Continue to a stile, to the left of a metal gate, and join the road at a three-way junction.

Turn right for a moment, then go straight ahead, ignoring the road which comes in from the right. Walk downhill for ¼ mile. First you will have woodland on either side, then you will pass a cluster of farm buildings on your left. The buildings soon give way to open fields. On your right you pass an old oast house, a cottage with hung tiles, then Pigdown Cottages and Farm. There should be a pond beside the road but this may well dry out in times of drought.

Go past the last cottage and turn right, where the garden ends, at the concrete 'public footpath' sign. Walk diagonally across the field to a stile a few paces to the right of the far corner. Cross into the next field and turn to look directly down over Hever village. These slopes, too, command good views over the surrounding countryside. Especially interesting is the cluster of stable buildings at Polebrook beside the Eden. As you go down, the inn appears clearly ahead of you.

To make your way downhill, walk past a small pond (which dries out

Hever Castle.

in summer) then go over a pair of stiles across a pathway running at right angles to the walk. You will see a culvert to your right which, though more like a dry ditch in summer, runs full of water after wet weather. Beside it grow mature hazel, rowan and oak. Follow the culvert round to the right and, 250 yards on, turn right, over a stile, through the hedge, onto a narrow road.

Turn left and when the road goes left, continue straight ahead into a metalled lane, marked by a sign which reads 'no horseriding'. Continue down this lane until you reach a point where a small field comes up in a wedge from the school. You will see the school and the broach spire of St Peter's church beyond, on your right.

Turn off the path into the field on your left. Cross the meadow section and the playing field and enter the car park of the King Henry VIII. The inn lies ahead.

Place of interest nearby

Hever Castle, a medieval moated manor house, was bought by Geoffrey Bullen, great-grandfather of Anne Boleyn in 1459. Several families owned it in the intervening centuries until the Astor family restored and developed it in the early 20th century. The castle is open daily from March to November. The gardens open at 11 am, the castle at 12 noon; last admission 5 pm, winter 4 pm. Telephone: 01732 865224.